T0209074

LIVING YOUR LEGACY
NOW!

Inspiring Life Lessons for a Successful, Healthy, and Fulfilling Life

BILL BLALOCK

ARCHWAY
PUBLISHING

Archway Publishing books may be ordered through booksellers or by contacting:

Archway Publishing
1663 Liberty Drive
Bloomington, IN 47403
www.archwaypublishing.com
844-669-3957

Because of the dynamic nature of the Internet, any web addresses or
links contained in this book may have changed since publication and
may no longer be valid. The views expressed in this work are solely those
of the author and do not necessarily reflect the views of the publisher,
and the publisher hereby disclaims any responsibility for them.

Any people depicted in stock imagery provided by Getty Images are
models, and such images are being used for illustrative purposes only.
Certain stock imagery © Getty Images.

ISBN: 978-1-6657-0136-5 (sc)
ISBN: 978-1-6657-0135-8 (hc)
ISBN: 978-1-6657-0137-2 (e)

Library of Congress Control Number: 2021900352

Print information available on the last page.

Archway Publishing rev. date: 04/23/2021

I'd rather be inspired to do or say something great in my life than be motivated to just do something.
—Bill Blalock

CONTENTS

INTRODUCTION

Living Your Legacy Now! is the product of my personal experiences and those shared by my clients, friends, and business associates. This is a comprehensive book of life lessons that will help you as you go through various experiences in your life!

Countless books, articles, and other media have been written about human behavior, leadership, success, and positive life balance. This book seeks to not be a duplication but a unique comprehensive reference book that will be a constant resource of encouragement and influence.

Living Your Legacy Now! contains topical life lessons that will give you a higher probability of success in your personal and professional life. They are simple by design, and the content is easy to understand, think through, and apply to your life. Life lessons range from defining truth, emotional moments, personal goals, being a person of influence and success, managing stress, mindfulness, and retirement.

By exercising these principles, you will have a higher probability of a positive life legacy now and in the future. People will long remember the impact you made on their lives.

May your journey through *Living Your Legacy Now!* be a positive learning and life application process. Refer to it often and share it with others. Enjoy and benefit!

WHY TRUTH?

Real truth, based on facts, will
ultimately overcome the perceived
truth one believes to be true.

W hen there is chaos, there is uncertainty. That's where we find ourselves when the very structures of government, truth, and decency seem to be vanishing. Aside from the day-to-day issues of life that we all live with, the external issues of life and making a living make it even more difficult to focus on what is important. You may ask, What do you mean? Simply stated, I mean the truth!

We need to stop, take a deep breath, and clear our minds of all the distractions that keep us from focusing on the truth. I was raised to tell the truth and abide by the laws of the land and the boundaries set down by my parents. It is only then that we can live in full confidence that we are doing and saying the right things. And when we cross the line, we reap the consequences.

Yes, I have crossed the line a time or two, but after the consequences were applied, I learned very quickly not to repeat those mistakes. When we live in truth, we can breathe easily with a sigh of relief and go about our daily living. As adults, we often need to do serious research to find truth in what we hear and see. That demands personal responsibility. Ultimately, it's up to you. I believe the world would be a better place if we all truly sought the truth in all matters of life and living!

So what exactly is the truth? In his *Baker Encyclopedia of Christian Apologetics,* Norman Geisler offers a helpful list of what truth is and what it is not. I base my following remarks on some points he has written.[1]

WHAT TRUTH IS NOT

1. Truth is not what works. *Pragmatism* says an idea is true if it works. Cheating and lying often work, but that does not make them true.

2. Truth is not what feels good. *Mysticism* and *subjectivism* both affirm personal feelings as the basis of truth. But feelings can be misleading. And if two persons' feelings conflict, who decides whose is true? Feelings may or may not correspond with what is true.

3. Truth is not whatever you want it to be. *Relativism* says that truth is whatever one declares it to be. But no one can live this way. If I say a traffic light is green when it is red, there will be serious consequences. As Daniel Patrick Moynihan said, "You're entitled to your own opinion, but you're not entitled to your own facts."

4. Truth is not just what we perceive with the senses. *Empiricism* says that only what we can measure empirically (with the five senses) is true. But truth is more than this. What about things like beauty and truth and justice and love? They cannot be discovered by the five senses. Plus, our senses can mislead us.

5. Truth is not what the majority believe. *Majoritarianism* says truth is what most people agree to. But the crowd can be wrong. Truth is not based on majority vote. Indeed, truth can easily not be known by the majority.

---

[1] [Norman Geisler, Baker Encyclopedia of Christian Apologetics, Baker Academic, a division of Baker Publishing Group, 5th Printing December 2000, Used by permission]

WHAT TRUTH IS

1. Truth is *universal*. Truth is something true for all people, for all places, for all times. Truth does not change among different cultures, different historical eras, or different nationalities.
2. Truth is *absolute*. It is not relative. An absolute is needed for standards. There can be no standards without absolutes. Indeed, there can be no measurement without absolutes.
3. Truth is *objective*. It is "independent of the knower and his consciousness," as Peter Kreeft and Ronald Tacelli put it. It is not based on subjective feelings or personal opinions. Truth does not reside in us or in our opinions. Personal experience is not the basis of truth. Truth is something that is external to us. We discover truth that already exists. We don't make it up or create it.
4. Truth *corresponds with reality*. It corresponds to the way things really are, to the actual being described. Truth is telling it like it is.
5. Truth is *personal*. Truth is more than just abstract theories and propositions. Truth is something that demands a personal response.
6. Truth is *knowable*. We may not know truth exhaustively, but we can know true truth.

Truth should never be mistaken for what it is not. Truth is, has been, and always will be truth!

Always seek truth. In so doing, you will gain much wisdom and peace in your life!

YOUR THOUGHTS

Mastery of self is the endless battle in which we must pursue our consciousness straight forward, and head over heels transmute all our focus on what it is ailing our immediate reality. Question yourself without pride and ego, step out of your shoes and look from the outside in. What do you see? What do you hear? This is the reflection your energy, your absolute control source. Does it benefit you?

—Will Barnes, *The Expansion of the Soul*

There is power in silence. Reflective thought brings life into focus. The key is conscious awareness. Ask yourself: Why do I think and feel the way I do? Thoughts and feelings are so interrelated. They are always connected in some form. Is there a better approach to resolving conflict or making significant changes in your life? Of course! As long as you are consciously aware of your thoughts and actions. Thinking before you speak or act a certain way is always a good decision.

When we bring conscious awareness to our decision-making processes and the ways we relate to our surroundings and individuals, we experience enhanced well-being.

Is it easy? Not always. But just as persistent physical exercise produces a healthy body and thus healthier living, persistent thoughtfulness produces a healthy mind and thus healthier consciousness. Thoughtfulness is always a better path than an emotional response. We have enough stimuli around us all the time to cause us to react and respond.

The benefits to individuals of raising their conscious awareness include:

- greater empathy toward others and their surroundings
- increased to wellness and healthy living
- improved consciousness, which adds to personal growth

- the ability to see things from different perspectives and then make wise, informed decisions
- an enhanced ability to filter out distractions in their thinking processes to arrive at new concepts, ideas, and solutions

If you choose to not be consciously aware, you will not achieve harmony with yourself because you will not clearly understand yourself. The result is you will not achieve harmony with other people.

You need to affirm and state that you intend to become more conscious and aware. When you initiate that commitment, act on it, and expand your consciousness, you will have a more balanced well-being.

By choosing to lie to yourself, to succumb to fear, to remain ignorant of knowledge, and so on, you put out the intention to lower your consciousness. And in so doing, you initiate a process that will attract more falsehood, fear, ignorance, and the like into your life.

Every thought you hold serves to either expand or contract your consciousness. There is no neutral. The decision is yours.

We need to consistently exercise conscious awareness as we deal with life events. In so doing, we will make better decisions that we can benefit from personally and professionally.

INTEGRITY

Be impeccable with your word. Speak with
integrity. Say only what you mean. Avoid
using the word to speak against yourself or
to gossip about others. Use the power of
your word in the direction of truth and love.

—Don Miguel Ruiz

W e are made strong in our weakness. Therefore, when we acknowledge our weakness, we can gain strength through knowledge and experience.

We are human and prone to make mistakes and at times offend people unintentionally. When these mistakes are brought to our attention, a sincere apology is always in order. A sincere apology clears the mind and soul of the offense and enriches the perception of the offended. Both are liberated.

Borrowing from the past to feed bitterness in the present is like pouring acid into an open wound. What do you expect to gain but more pain? Let the past be the past and let go of the present moment of discontent.

There is always more positive energy to draw from in life; do not feed the flame of destructive thoughts and emotions!

Words are very powerful. When they are spoken, you cannot take them back. As defined by the dictionary, integrity is "the quality of possessing and steadfastly adhering to high moral principles or professional standards, and the state of being complete, undivided, sound or undamaged." Integrity, then, is having high principles and standards in your life that are consistent with who you truly are!

Don't use language carelessly. Choose your words carefully.

We all consider ourselves to be good people; however, we choose on occasion to not be totally truthful because we either do not want to offend someone or we truly don't want to respond to an invitation in the affirmative. When others hear us and accept untruths as normal behavior, is that a good thing? How many times have you been invited to an event and your response was, "Sorry, but we already have plans on that day," when in truth, you had no plans at all on that day? You just did not want to go because of the type of occasion or because you were not fond of the person extending the invitation. Essentially, you were not truthful! Therein lies a lack of integrity.

If your friends or children see you consistently responding in this way, they know that your response is not truthful. You have acted as if your deficiency in speaking truthfully is normal behavior. Therefore, you are not being truthful.

Ask yourself, what would be a more appropriate response? Can you relate to these examples?

- Your phone rings, and another family member answers, but you don't want to talk to them? What do you do? "Tell them I am not here."
- You get into an argument and say, "I'm not mad. I'm just upset with what happened today at work."
- A friend calls and asks if you can come over and help them with a project, and you say, "I'll be right over a few minutes." And you then proceed to run a few errands and arrive an hour later!
- A friend calls and leaves a message or sends and email that they need to talk to you ASAP and either your "forget to respond" or respond two days later.

Dependence on a false statement to create comfort within ourselves or not to offend others can deeply affect our ability to be true to our word and our sense of personal integrity. Others begin to think that those untruths or lack of response are acceptable behavior, and they become the norm. This is not a good thing!

Honesty and integrity go hand in hand!

To have integrity is to be a complete person: honest, truthful, and with consistently high moral standards. To live without integrity is to be an incomplete person. Dishonesty retards both our personal and social development. It causes us to fall short of realizing our full potential for our lives with inner peace, feelings of self-worth, and healthy relationships.

When you speak, whether good news or bad, speak in the direction of truth and love. Ask yourself: Is what I am saying truthful? Is it necessary? Is what I am saying kind and enduring to the person I am talking to?

It is essential to be truthful to others as well as yourself. All too often, we convince ourselves—justify our thinking and actions—when we know what we are saying and/or doing is wrong. Don't lie to yourself. Have integrity within yourself as well as with others.

Time to take inventory:

- Where are you in or out of integrity? (Consider family, work, relationships, personal and professional priorities, money, health, and welfare.)

- How can you improve in your integrity? How would it feel when you make needed adjustments and reestablish integrity in your life?
- What mistaken belief systems or excuses are you currently using, which do not contribute to your personal integrity? What is it costing you and others when you are not a person of integrity?

So, when there is a misunderstanding and an offense has been experienced, exercise vigilance and clear the air as soon as possible. Be truthful and forthcoming in all your communications. Exercise good judgment as you make adjustments in your life to build your personal integrity. Reaffirm understanding and enhance your business and personal relationships with a good dose of integrity!

Others will not forget—they will remember!

GOING TO THE EXTREME

Extremism is so easy. You've got your position, and that's it. It doesn't take much thought. And when you go far enough to the right, you meet the same idiots coming around from the left.

—Clint Eastwood

W e continue to hope for reasonable people to discuss issues at hand with civility and intellect to the point that each party to the conversation clearly understands their differences and can arrive at a consensus for the benefit of all. We will not always agree, but we can be agreeable on a direction. If one disagrees with an ideology or a political or theological position, that individual needs to be prepared to propose an alternative position that is fully documented and supported.

All too often, people just believe what they hear and don't test the information with verifying evidence. We tend to react and respond rather than thinking with a purpose! Extreme positions of thought and action can produce casualties on both sides of the spectrum.

Remember, we are what we think—and the way we think determines how we experience life and where we go with it. Therefore, if we want to change our lives, we first need to change our thinking.

When was the last time you made an important decision in your life, solved a complex problem, created an innovation, thought about the purpose of your life, or planned for something big? How long did you spend on that?

One useful way to answer these questions is to start by describing why we think and what purpose it serves for us. If we examine the reasons behind the thinking process, we can better understand how thinking can be helpful in our lives.

TO MAKE DECISIONS

Making decisions is perhaps one of the most legitimate reasons for thinking. We have choices. We think about alternative courses of action—and then we decide to go for one of them. Simple? Looks like it. That's basically how we make simple decisions like what we are going to wear for the day or evening or if we are going to eat at home or go out for dinner. We also make complex decisions in the same manner. We define a problem or situation, identify various options, apply a thinking process, choose one option, and go for it.

TO SOLVE PROBLEMS

Being able to solve problems requires serious thought. Doctors solve problems every day by diagnosing diseases and treating them. Coaches and consultants do pretty much the same thing; the difference is that their clients are businesses or individuals instead of patients in need of a doctor's diagnosis. In the same manner, counselors and psychologists encourage the thought process as their clients go through therapy.

There are also plenty of examples of problem-solving in everyday life: how to get through heavy traffic and get to a destination on time, how to get out of an unpleasant situation, or how to avoid a certain person as much as possible. Solving problems, which requires thinking, is part of everyday life, and it may be part of one's job too. So it's very beneficial to become good at it since it can differentiate us from others who are less skilled in solving problems.

TO CREATE SOMETHING NEW

Creating a new app, programming software, writing a novel, creating another work of art, making a film, and designing a building are all examples of creativity and innovation. It is the type of thinking that creates something where nothing previously existed. Literary works, arts, and musical masterpieces are made because of thinking in creative ways.

How about creating a new life for yourself? We may need to think creatively about ourselves on occasion. Envisioning what we want to do in the future and where we are going in our life or career often requires creative thinking. In other words, it's all about imagining a state of being that doesn't exist right now—or one that exists only as a possibility—and then envisioning how we might make it happen somewhere down the line.

Creativity is an integral ingredient of higher thinking for any reason or purpose. Thinking with a purpose is powerful!

TO UNDERSTAND SOMETHING

Thinking is a great way to understand things. There are plenty of ways to create understanding, but we can categorize them into three main groups.

MAKING ASSOCIATIONS

How is one concept, theory, or idea related to another? Are they related in some way? One process of thought leads us to consider another course of action or theory.

MAKING JUDGMENTS

Is what I am thinking a "good" thing or a "bad" thing? Making judgments is a way of thinking that puts a positive or negative value or label on everything we see, hear, or think about. It's like making an association with a positive or negative value judgment attached to it.

MAKING CONCLUSIONS

For every cause, there is an effect! What will happen if I make a specific decision in my life or think a certain way? These conclusions utilize logical thinking, and they are generally based on what we assume or have seen or experienced in the past. Making sound conclusions is not always easy, and anyone can fall into the trap of making a conclusion based on what they want to see instead of basing it on sound judgment and what the facts tell. It is so important to be mindful of the facts when we are deciding or arriving at a certain opinion.

Set aside some time often to just think and contemplate in a free-flowing process. Have no definitive decision or thought process in mind. Be open to your thoughts and creative visions. Opportunities for free-flowing thought can enhance creativity and give rise to new undiscovered possibilities in life.

Voltaire got it right long ago: "Those who can make you believe absurdities can make you commit atrocities." Bertrand Russell did too: "Many people would sooner die than think; in fact, they do."

What are you thinking through today?

WHAT HAPPENS WHEN YOU FAIL?

Far better is it to dare mighty things,
to win glorious triumphs, even though
checkered by failure ... than to rank with
those poor spirits who neither enjoy nor
suffer much, because they live in a gray
twilight that knows not victory nor defeat.

—Theodore Roosevelt

"**W**hat went wrong?" We have all asked that question from time to time. After all, part of the success formula is *failure*. So what do you do and how do you feel when you fail? Here are some helpful insights:

1. *Being optimistic, which is a great personal quality, opens the opportunity to make errors in the process.* Accept the fact that your personality lends itself to look for new ways of doing things and that, in the process, you will fail at some, but succeed in most. We often dwell on our past successes or past failures. This is a very common practice of many of us. When we do that, we live in the past. We need to be focused on the future and always moving forward. Say to yourself: "It's another day, and I am getting up and moving on in my life."

2. *Enjoy the fact that you will learn from your mistakes and continue to grow and improve your life.* We all make mistakes. Think about what led to the mistake you made. What was your mental and emotional state of mind at that time? Many decisions are made out of fear. If that's the case, reflect on what generated that fear and what emotion you were experiencing. Be consciously aware of that emotion, and the next time it surfaces, address it, accept it, and bypass it. Avoid making the same mistake again.

3. *Always remember that failure is usually a prelude to success.* Why? Well, the more you try, the more you perfect the process or product you are developing. Steve Jobs, Elon Musk, Bill Gates, and Mark Zuckerberg are prime examples.

4. *Ask for advice from a trusted colleague or mentor.* Learn from their mistakes and what they learned through their experiences. Asking can be difficult, but it is necessary to gain insight and knowledge. Remember, knowledge is power, and that energy will propel you to reframe every thought and action, so you make the best choices and do not fail again.

5. *Don't be fearful—be fearless!* Fearlessness is not the absence of fear; it's the mastery of fear. Fearlessness is about getting up one more time than we fall. The more comfortable we are with the possibility of falling, the more fearless we will be! Without fear, we can't have courage. We cannot act courageous in any situation unless we have something to protect of value, something to honor, something to prove or defend, or something to commit to. Fear is a call to action to be courageous and above all fearless!

6. *Pace yourself.* Learn to let go, regroup, and try again! Mistakes are inevitable. We all make mistakes. Stepping away and taking some time to regroup is usually best. Take a day off, schedule a vacation, or simply go for a walk and reflect on all your options and chart a new course in your decision-making process.

7. *Never blame others for your misfortunes or mistakes.* Own them! If we have offended another by our words or actions, we should make it right. We must change our behavior. This

means communicating to the person who was affected that you were at fault. It also means, where appropriate, making your confession in public.

8. *Never wait for the right moment—sometimes tomorrow never comes—and you miss the opportunity.* Take definitive action and make it right as soon as you can!

Try as you will, you will sometimes fail, but you are not a failure. Keep focused, be diligent, and seek to accomplish the goals you have set for yourself.

Remember, some of the best lessons we ever learn are learned from past mistakes. The error of the past is the wisdom and success for your future.

GENEROSITY

All our relationships are person-to-person.
They involve people seeing, hearing, touching,
and speaking to each other; they involve
sharing goods; and they involve moral
values like generosity and compassion.

—Brendan Myers

enerosity is a selfless act of love. It is what life is all about. The act of giving generously strengthens your self-esteem, increases your religious faith, and will lengthen your life! It is not always an actual giving of a material item or financial contribution, although these are good actions on your part.

Generous people are healthier and more satisfied with life than those who don't give. It produces within us a sense that we can make a difference in this world and shows that we are actively addressing the needs of those around us.

Think about some ways you can express generosity today!

- Practice the art of gratitude in your life. Think more about how you have been blessed and less about what you don't have or have not accomplished. When you realize how good your life is, you will want to share it with others and not be so self-focused.

- Compliment and congratulate those who have achieved success in a task or career. Recall the moment you received a compliment or got a promotion. It felt good that others took notice and celebrated your success. Extend to them the same congratulatory remarks and encourage them in their new opportunity.

- Encourage others in their life walk—in good times and bad. We all have memorable moments and occasions we want to forget. Be available to your friends and others and express words of encouragement in their successes. And to those who are going through a difficult situation—personal or professional—be there for them. Listen a lot, give assurances that time will heal, and let them know personally that you are there for them.

- Give your time and resources to institutions, organizations, and causes that you truly believe in! Getting out in your community and expressing interest in causes you believe in is important for your personal growth. Whether it is through your political, religious, or social contacts, get involved.

- Refocus on your financial giving to worthy causes. Make a point to give each month *before* you begin spending. In that way, you will practice the art of giving on a consistent basis. The practice of giving *after* our spending is unfortunately common practice. If we don't do it first, we may not give at all. Every gift—whether great or small—instills in you a heart for and practice of generosity.

- Spend time with generous people. Ask them the ultimate questions: Why are you so generous? How did you start? What motivates you to give? What advice would you give a person who wants to be more generous? Generous persons are the best role models. Model your actions after them.

- Love yourself generously and others unconditionally. Loving ourselves is an intentional decision that we make. By loving ourselves, we have the unique capacity to love others unconditionally. The choice is yours. The amazing result of practicing generosity and unconditional love in your life is that it is returned to you many times over—freely and without asking!

LOYALTY

The foundation stones for a balanced
success are honesty, character,
integrity, faith, love, and loyalty.

—Zig Ziglar

Remember those who have been loyal to you:

- To those who have gone to the next level in their career thanks to the referral and support of a trusted colleague, be loyal!

- To those who continue to build financial wealth at the direction of a trusted professional, be loyal!

- To those who have experienced substantial spiritual growth by the influence of a friend, mentor, or minister, be loyal!

- To those who experience good health and wellness at the direction of a trainer, wellness coach, or physician, be loyal!

- To those who support you when you are at your lowest emotional level or feelings of abandonment, be loyal!

- To those who love you for who you are, be loyal!

Always be thankful and stay close to those individuals who have had faith in you, stood by you, and worked with your best interest in mind. These individuals are gems, and they are hard to find! Stay with them and support them as well.

Remember to be loyal to yourself:

- Know who you are. What makes you happy and engaged in your everyday living.

- Like yourself. Being kind, forgiving, and generous to yourself gives you power within yourself to acknowledge your accomplishments when others don't. Your self-talk reaffirms the value you see in yourself: "I am a good person." "I do great work." "I care about my friends and treat them with respect."

- You care how you feel about yourself. You are not too concerned about how everyone else is feeling. This is not to be perceived as being vain; it is an acknowledgment within yourself that you really do care about how you feel.

- You are honest and straightforward about your feelings to others. When you do this, you become an authentic person. Others know exactly what you think and feel about a certain topic or situation. At the same time, you allow others to be loyal to themselves. You accept their diversity of thought and actions even if they are contrary to yours.

Always be loyal to those who have helped you along life's journey—and always be loyal to yourself. This is a winning combination!

CRISIS SITUATIONS

Meanings are not determined by
situations, but we determine ourselves
by the meanings we give to situations.

—Unknown

A t different points in life, events that we do not expect give us a jolt and make us wonder if we will ever recover, but they are just events in time. Some are cyclical, and some are truly life changing. You may relate to these examples:

- Your spouse wants a divorce, a long-standing friendship ends, or you are betrayed by a business partner.
- Your physician tells you that you have cancer, an incurable disease, or a medical condition that necessitates surgery.
- Your company terminates or outplaces you.
- The stock market makes an abrupt significant drop—when it's only a "correction" and will recover over time!
- A child or family member has a substance abuse problem.
- A family member or close friend dies.
- Your business is failing and headed for bankruptcy.
- You find yourself in excess debt.

Each of these events gives cause for us to draw from our inner strength, our spiritual and emotional core! I can personally relate to some of these events, and I am sure you have as well. In retrospect, we realize that we did make it through and became stronger in the process. Make sure you are grounded in your personal faith and have a support system of close friends and family.

Here are some helpful coping suggestions that can help when going through a crisis:

DON'T FOOL YOURSELF

When you are faced with hard times and difficult circumstances, don't try to convince yourself that nothing negative and destructive is happening in your life. Pretending is not a good idea! Accept that fact that you are at a crisis point in your life that will be painful. Accepting doesn't change the circumstances, but it does relieve added pressure that you don't need.

ACCEPT BEING OVERWHELMED

You may feel overwhelmed, but don't bottle up your emotions. Emotions are powerful. Express them rather than withholding within. Check that you don't think and use the "always" and "never" terminology when addressing the crisis. If you do, you will be leaning toward catastrophizing. Remember, whatever is happening is not the end of the world. You need to turn off this type of thinking and speaking. We usually bounce back after a crisis.

PRACTICE CONTROLLED BREATHING

Being in a fight-or-flight mode inhibits our ability to help solve a crisis. Your body has the capacity to help. Rapid breathing only increases cortisol, the stress hormone. It just gets worse. By regulating your breathing, you slowly reduce your level of stress. Take in slow, deep breaths and release them slowly. Mentally tell yourself to relax. You can handle this. Repeat as needed to reach a calmer state. You can then think more clearly as a result of increasing the oxygen level in your bloodstream. It would also be a good thing to do some research on meditation, yoga, or a regular exercise program, which will greatly help you through periods of crisis and uncertainty.

FOCUS ON FAITH

Elizabeth Lesser, author of *Broken Open: How Difficult Times Can Help Us Grow*, says, "Faith involves trusting that whatever is happening has a meaning and purpose. Even hard times can teach us something. Having faith loosens our need to control the outcome of life, which is good because it's impossible to control something as unruly as life anyway."

Adversity has a way of creating resiliency, strength, and increased faith and purpose for every person who completes the journey through a crisis. Having made it through the crisis, we are well equipped when the next unexpected event comes our way.

If you find yourself in a crisis point in your life, and these personal coping suggestions don't help significantly, seek the counsel of professionals to help you in your journey. Seek out a professional licensed counselor or psychologist. Do not isolate yourself. Remind yourself that you are a person of value! If you know of someone going through a crisis event in their lives, be there for them and help them seek the help they need.

Charles R. Swindoll said, "We are all faced with a series of great opportunities brilliantly disguised as impossible situations."

JUDGING

If we are honest with ourselves, we have to admit that sometimes our assumptions and preconceived notions are wrong, and therefore, our interpretation of events is incorrect. This causes us to overreact, to take things personally, or to judge people unfairly.

—Elizabeth Thornton

J udging is more pervasive in our culture than ever. In degrees, it breaks down relationships and creates barriers to understanding. Here are some areas that affect us individually and how we view others:

- the media (publications, radio, TV, internet, and social media)
- clothing
- speech
- education
- political ideology
- religion/faith
- race/nationality
- social class
- sexual orientation
- geographic location
- organizations and affiliations

We need to examine our reactions to how we perceive others and realize that at the end of the day, it goes both ways. We are always being viewed—judged—by other people as well. The best application of our energy is to realize that we will not always agree with another person or group—just as they can learn to tolerate us.

How can we become less judgmental?

1. Take a pause before passing judgment. When someone's behavior is offensive, or we feel threatened, we don't readily see the reasons for their behavior. Try to get some understanding of their actions before your make a judgment.

2. Always be mindful of your own actions. See if you can understand where the other person may be coming from. Remember that words spoken can never be taken back!

3. Don't take it "personal." When someone disagrees with you, depersonalize it as best you can. Their actions may be the result of their own pain or personal struggles. Remember: everyone is dealing with something or someone in their lives.

4. If offended, use 'I" statements instead of "you" statements when confronting the individual. Instead of saying, *"You always act in an offensive manner,"* try saying, *"I feel frustrated when you ..."* The "I" expression lets the other person know how the behavior or language affects you personally. Such a response may well cause the other person to reevaluate their actions and make needed changes, turning a negative into a positive learning experience. I refer to this as "creative criticism" in the form of a future request for improved behavior in the future.

5. Educate yourself! Always remember it is not about you! There may be physical or emotional reasons. They may suffer from ADD, ADHD, Asperger's syndrome, or some other condition. Some people just have poor social skills or

lack knowledge in certain areas that would cause them to act the way they do.

One common thread that we can all subscribe to is accepting the fact that we are all different and must, in a community, seek understanding and acceptance of others and our differences. We may express frustration at times, but we need to keep focused on accepting others as they are, living our own lives reflecting dignity and character, doing no harm, and accepting others as they go through life's journey.

WHAT ARE YOUR REGRETS?

I try to live my life where I end up at a point where I have no regrets. So I try to choose the road that I have the most passion on because then you can never really blame yourself for making the wrong choices. You can always say you're following your passion.

—Darren Aronofsky

T hroughout life, we will have opportunities to address areas of potential regret. Everyone wants to live a life of fulfillment. There are areas where we can fall short of the best life has to offer. Here are some regrets that you may have and how to address them.

NOT HAVING MEANINGFUL RELATIONSHIPS

First, you need to have the desire to connect with other people. Realize that you are not an island unto yourself. You are a part of community—and you need to act on your desire to connect with others. Think of the people you spend time with. Over time, someone special may surface who you really feel a connection to. It could be your future life partner.

Second, spend real time together! Sure, we can use social media, emails, text messages, phone calls, FaceTime, Zoom, or Skype, but there is no substitution for face-to-face time together. Make a real connection. Meet for coffee, schedule lunch, go for a walk, visit a museum, or just agree to go somewhere special. Discover common interests.

Third, demonstrate the effort and express your caring and commitment to individuals who bring joy, meaning, and purpose to your life. Share your life experiences and common interests with persons who are special to you.

How many times have you had a relationship that lasted for years and you knew in your heart that you wanted to spend your life with that particular person, but you held back because you did not want to make yourself vulnerable and open? You passed up many such relationships and now find yourself alone. Is that what you want out of life? We all want to be loved. So crash the "barrier of the self," share your life and love with that one person, and experience a mutual respect and love for each other! Do not regret the beauty of being in love and being loved by another person!

You may find that one person you desire to spend your life with. On the other hand, you may be a person who does not desire a permanent relationship such as marriage, but you enjoy the company of a particular person and circle of friends with common interests. There is nothing wrong with that. The key is to connect. As a result, you will share times of joy and sadness, celebrate special occasions, take trips, take up new interests, and experience a life of caring and commitment.

NOT SPENDING TIME WITH YOUR FAMILY

This is a tough one. With family members relocating because of career choices, we find ourselves physically distant from our siblings and parents. Physical distance can be overcome by internet communications, Facetime, Skype, Zoom, regular phone calls, or actual visits. If your family members are in the same city, invite them over for dinner occasionally—not just the holidays—or go to a special game or event in your city. If you have grandchildren, make sure you make yourself available to attend their sporting events, concerts, and special school events. Staying connected is so especially important. Moments with members of your family are to be cherished. Make a special effort to connect with your parents as they age. Redeem every moment with them. There will come a time when all you will have is memories!

Never use the excuse that you don't have the time! All you really have is time. So make magic moments that you will remember!

HAVE POOR MENTAL HEALTH

Many people live with undiagnosed low-level depression that emerges in their twenties and thirties and accelerates as they age. Some self-medicate their conditions with drugs and alcohol initially and then become victims of poor life choices and bad career moves. Undiagnosed mental health results in increased self-doubt. Some never recover. If you sense something is wrong, be honest with yourself and get professional help. Act and seek the help you need from a psychologist or licensed professional counselor (LPC).

NOT TAKING ADVANTAGE OF EDUCATION

With continued advances in technology and changes in the workforce, ongoing education is a necessity. We have always placed a value on a college education, but that is not always necessary for a person to have a successful career. After high school, technical schools or junior colleges are excellent resources for learning skills that can result in a good-paying job or even be the foundation for a person's own business, such as plumbing, carpentry, cooking, computer software development, or coding. Many learned skills also have certification and licensing programs to further enhance their value in the workforce. The emphasis on continuing education is a must.

Many professions require a college degree. Some examples are accounting, teaching, psychology, physician's assistant, health care, professional golf management, law/political science, and engineering. Advanced degrees can be obtained locally or via long-distance learning through accredited universities. It can be accomplished while you are still working. Night, weekend, and online courses provide flexibility for obtaining an advanced education.

Always remember, once you start the process, never stop. If you only take one or two courses per quarter or semester, keep the momentum going. Do not stop until you have obtained your degree! Then comes ongoing continued education and needed certifications for your specific career field.

Education is not an option. We should always seek new knowledge and skills that will lead to a more fulfilling and productive life. Take steps now to make it happen in your life if you have not already!

NOT BEING CHARITABLE

The best in life is achieved when we share our time and our resources with others. It is through giving that we build self-esteem. When you help others, you will find yourself not dwelling on your own issues and concerns of life. Building meaningful relationships with family members and friends as well as mentoring others will add meaning and purpose to your life. It will give you perspective and enhance your quality of life. Give and you will receive!

NOT HAVING SPECIAL INTERESTS

Is there something you have always wanted to do? Sign up for piano lessons, art or painting classes, or voice lessons, sing in a church choir or local civic music choral, play in an orchestra, or join a theater group. How about taking up golf or tennis, participating in an exercise class, or joining a book club? There may be areas of interest that you have done in the past but not continued or areas of your life that you want to learn and experience for the first time. Do you want to explore and learn something new and refreshing? Only you can answer that question. It will make your life more fulfilling and satisfied!

NOT LIVING YOUR FAITH

Your religious faith is the foundation of your life. It is through faith that we experience a connection with the Divine. The fact that there is a God who loves you and desires to have a relationship with you is priceless. The fellowship of other believers in your faith circle provides emotional and spiritual support through your life challenges. The security that your faith gives you is eternal. After this life, we have the hope of an eternal life. Connect with your faith. Attend services regularly, volunteer, and be active. Friends who share the same faith are extremely valuable in an impersonal and detached world. Practice and live your faith!

NOT LIVING A HEALTHY LIFESTYLE

Are you exercising, eating good nutritious food, and getting adequate rest? If you are not, chances are you have a weight problem, and it is possible that you do not have a healthy self-image. Obesity and being overweight are conditions that are pervasive in our society. It is a global problem. More importantly, it is a personal problem for those who refuse to address their weight. If you want to run the risk of high blood pressure, high cholesterol, gout, heart problems, exhaustion, and other maladies, then do nothing! As you get older, it is much more difficult to lose the weight and be healthy. The decision is yours. Seek guidance from your doctor, a dietitian, and a certified trainer. Hopefully, you will take positive action now that could result in adding years to your life!

WORRY

It has been proven that we spend too much time worrying about things and life events that never come to fruition. If you are in the habit of worrying obsessively, it is difficult to break out of that habit. Resolve to break this addiction! Remember:

- The future can never be predicted. So quit trying to control what you cannot.
- Live in the moment. There is no reality to the images you create in your mind. Worry only serves to make you feel bad.
- Your mind is not in control. Life is a continuum, constantly changing. The only moment you are in control of is the present moment. What you are worrying about does not really exist as anything other than a thought or idea. Live in the moment! As a result, you will be healthier and happier!

This is not a complete list. However, remember that regrets in the present can be addressed and converted into positive streams of energy, resulting in fewer regrets as we face the later parts of our lives.

When we are faced with the fact that life is ending, and we will soon be dying, life takes on a completely new perspective. How would we live differently if we had the chance? At that point, we do not have the time—only regrets!

Bonnie Ware, an Australian nurse, wrote about the top regrets[2] of the dying:

- I wish I had the courage to live a life true to myself, not the life others expected of me. (This was the most common regret.)
- I wish I hadn't worked so hard.
- I wish I had the courage to express my feelings.
- I wish I had stayed in touch with my friends.
- I wish I let myself be happier.

Do you relate to any of the regrets mentioned or the themes expressed by Ms. Ware? Would you not want to live life now—while you still have time—than to have regrets in the future? What is your greatest regret? What will you set out to achieve or change before your own demise?

---

[2] *The Guardian*, February 1, 2012.

ME TIME!

The greatest omission in American life is solitude; not loneliness, for this is alienation that thrives most during crowds, but that zone of time and space free from outside pressure which is the incubator of the spirit.

—Marya Mannes

t is good to take an occasional sabbatical to regroup and contemplate your future initiatives. Discover the benefits of taking time out for yourself. Experience the value of solitude in your life. I have discovered the benefits of taking some time to reflect.

You cannot always be on task! You need a brain rest with no distractions. It enables you to focus and think more clearly. Disconnect to connect within. Find a quiet place, turn off external distractions—cell phone, internet, TV, pager, radio, or anything that you would define as distracting—close your eyes, and rest and reflect.

Getting up early in the morning is a winning strategy! Mornings are usually the most peaceful time of day. Your thought process will be more focused.

Gain a better understanding of yourself. You find your own voice and can express what you truly believe in rather than following the influence of a group or public opinion.

You work through problems more effectively when you are not distracted by incoming information—whether they are electronic, individual, or group influences.

You gain a better understanding of what you truly desire in life. As a result, you will make better choices. You also appreciate more your relationships with your spouse or partner and others.

Matthew Bowker, a psychoanalytic political theorist at Medaille College in Rochester, New York, has done some notable research on solitude. He contends that solitude is more than just being alone. It is a deeper internal process. Solitude requires internal exploration, which can be an uncomfortable process. "It might take a little bit of work before it turns into a pleasant experience. When experienced, it becomes the most important relationship you will ever have."

Solitude is a relationship with yourself that lifts you to a new level of self-reflection and understanding.

In *A Dangerous Place to Be: Identity, Conflict, and Trauma in Higher Education*, an upcoming book Matthew Bowker coauthored with David Levine, a psychoanalyst at the University of Denver, the authors trace a line between the devaluing of solitude and the ongoing ideological conflicts afflicting college campuses. "We're drawn to identity-markers and to groups that help us define [ourselves]. In the simplest terms, this means using others to fill out our identities, rather than relying on something internal, something that comes from within."

The discussion of "groups" in a university setting referenced by Bowker and Levine is applicable in all life settings. Groups have a powerful impact on defining who we are as individuals and how we relate to others in society.

Solitude is self-strengthening. You must have that capacity to know that you're going to be okay—and who you are does not need to be supported by a group identity. A healthy state of solitude supports the theory that you can be alone and not lonely!

The difference between solitude as rejuvenation and solitude as suffering is the quality of self-reflection that one can generate while in it, and the ability to come back to social groups when one wants to.

Solitude can be restorative when it is your choice, your setting, and your timing! It is necessary for a truly healthy mind and helps you understand yourself.

Any time is better than no time. So make time for yourself daily! Look at "your time" as a reward! It's your time for peace and solitude in a hectic and fast-paced world.

You are a good person and are worthy of taking care of yourself. So taking time out will boost your physical and mental well-being as well as increase your self-esteem!

WHERE IS TRUE HAPPINESS?

It isn't what you have or who you are or where you are or what you are doing that makes you happy or unhappy. It is what you think about it.

—Dale Carnegie, *How to Win Friends and Influence People*

have never met a person who does not want to be happy. We all do! So why is it that for some people, they are constantly seeking happiness? Are they looking in the wrong place? What does it take? When is enough *enough*?

- We must ask ourselves what makes us happy. Is it people/ relationships, material things, faith, or activities and organizations? This is a good place to start.

- Do you want to just survive or thrive? Do what you are passionate about, do what you do well, and love what you do! What tools do you need to accomplish that? What change needs to take place?

- What is your comfort zone? Do you feel good about what you are doing and where you are in your life's journey, profession, or relationship? Good feelings result when we are in our comfort zones.

If you keep wanting more in your life, *more* will never be enough for you to experience happiness in your life.

Philosophers, theologians, psychologists, and even economists have long sought to define it, and since the 1990s, a whole branch of psychology—positive psychology—has been dedicated to pinning it down and propagating it. More than simply positive mood, happiness is a state of well-being that encompasses living a good life—that is, with a sense of meaning and deep satisfaction.

Research shows that happiness is not the result of bouncing from one joy to the next; achieving happiness typically involves times of considerable discomfort. Money is important to happiness, but only to a certain point. Money buys freedom from worry about the basics in life—housing, food, and clothing—but genetic makeup, life circumstances, achievements, marital status, social relationships, and even your neighbors all influence how happy you are or can be.

We all have different ways of thinking and expressing feelings. Researchers estimate that much of happiness is under personal control. Regularly indulging in small pleasures (such as warm baths), getting absorbed in challenging activities, setting and meeting goals, maintaining close social ties, and finding purpose beyond oneself are all actions that increase life satisfaction.

So where lies the answer? It is *within* you!

First, be content and thankful where you are in the present moment. Express heartfelt gratitude. I truly believe that our sense of contentment only comes when we are spiritually grounded and connected. Only then does your perspective change and you become a thankful person. You think differently, but it does not stop there.

Secondly, we then press on; moving forward in our lives, we experience new opportunities. Never look back on past failures! New skills, degrees, relationships, activities, and material possessions will only supplement your happiness state of mind. They will not be the determining factors in your happiness.

At certain points in life, we have made more money and had more possessions, and there have been times when we just barely got by. In every situation, we adjusted and made the best decisions possible—in good times and bad. Hope lives within you because you are grounded in faith and trust in a faithful God with the support of friends and in many cases a loving and supportive family.

Happiness is not something you postpone for the future; it is something you design for the present.

Possessions, people, activities, and organizations will come and go, but one's relationship with themselves and, in many cases, with a loving and caring God makes the difference! Where are you in your journey for true happiness?

> Today I choose life. Every morning when I wake up, I can choose joy, happiness, negativity, pain. To feel the freedom than comes from being able to continue to make mistakes and choices—today I choose to feel life, not to deny my humanity but embrace it.
>
> —Kevyn Aucoin

SELF-ESTEEM

There is overwhelming evidence that the higher the level of self-esteem, the more likely one will be to treat others with respect, kindness, and generosity.

—Nathaniel Branden

aving a high sense of self-esteem is essential. So how do you build self-esteem? The key is *avoiding* those things in your life that repress your potential for a healthy sense of self.

SOME THINGS TO CONSIDER

- Focus on yourself. Don't compare yourself to other people.

- Encourage and celebrate the success of others. Don't put people down for their accomplishments or failures.

- You don't need to do everything perfectly! Don't obsess over making everything "perfect." Perfectionism results in disappointment most of the time.

- We are not perfect. Don't dwell on your failures in life. They are only moments in time. Learn from them and move on!

- Love yourself! Don't feel guilty about taking care of yourself.

- Do what makes you happy—as long as you don't break a law or hurt someone! Don't try to please other people all the time. Enjoy life!

- Be confident. Don't hold back your feelings. Engage people in conversation and learn from them.

- Move on! Don't spend your energy trying to "belong." Be yourself and set your own path that others will follow!

- Talk to yourself in a confident manner. Don't seek recognition. It will come naturally as you display confidence in your decision-making.

- Press on! Don't be bogged down with doubts and complaints. Don't be lazy! Be productive and active—and get the job done!

- Trust yourself! Don't wait on the sidelines for something to happen. Take some risks. Learn a new hobby or sport, change careers, or make a move!

- Stay out of other people's affairs! Don't involve yourself in another people's business! Stay focused on yourself and what you are involved in.

Self-esteem is respecting yourself! These four basic life elements will ensure you to have healthy self-esteem:

- *Be kind.* How can you feel good about yourself if you are mean, selfish, or insensitive? How we deal with other people has a mirror effect. It reflects on us. The better we treat others, the better we feel about ourselves.

- *Be honorable.* There is a connection between honesty and self-esteem. Integrity is the cornerstone of high self-esteem. As long as you have integrity, you will always be respected by others and by yourself. Honesty is still the best policy!

- *Be productive.* Don't be lazy! Being productive—learning, planning, achieving—is what builds self-esteem. There is never a substitute for hard work.

- *Be positive.* We can't feel good about ourselves if our heads a full of negative thoughts. If we are treating others with respect, are honest with ourselves and others, and are achieving something worthy in our lives, we need to give ourselves credit for it! It's healthy to have a good, positive attitude about ourselves. Remember, attitude is a choice!

Self-esteem is essential for achieving success in life. Believe in yourself and move on to higher levels of success. People with low self-esteem always feel a sense of entitlement. Decide today that your goal is to have a higher sense of self-worth and accomplishment in your life!

OVERCOMING FAILURE

Every individual suffers from the fear of failure, but you can change your destiny only when you overcome it.

—Anupam Kher

esilience is true happiness! We usually view successful people with admiration, but we need to realize that the journey to greatness took them through many negative experiences and possible failures. Life does throw all of us curve balls at times, but it's how we play the pitch!

- Throughout life, we will continue to experience positive and negative emotions because of our life experiences. You need to acknowledge the event and experience what you are feeling at that point in time. Acknowledge the sadness of the occasion, but express gratitude for this life experience because you are learning how to live!

- Be optimistic! When you face a challenge, don't say to yourself that you have no choice because "this is the only thing I can do!" Be creative and have alternative plans.

- Choose to "reject rejection." You do not have to be a prisoner of your own self-defeating thoughts.

- Have strong support systems! Find resources to help you get back on your feet when you get knocked down! Having a good social support system can boost your resilience to stress.

- Notice and appreciate the little things. When you do this consistently, you realize that "everything" is not going wrong in your life

- Seek out opportunities for growth and learning. "As a sense of competence increases, individuals are better able to respond effectively in unfamiliar or challenging situations and persevere in the face of failures and challenges," Kathleen M. Sutcliffe and Timothy J. Vogus write in *Organizing for Resilience*. "Setbacks and challenges can be our most powerful learning opportunities."

- Be relentlessly grateful! Gratitude is known to boost health and well-being. You have a higher probability of experiencing better physical health and mood than those who focus on hassles and complaints.

Choose this day to live a resilient and grateful life. When you do, you will experience successful living!

REFRAME YOUR LIFE!

My life has been filled with terrible misfortunes, most of which have never happened.

—Mark Twain

t's not so much what is said—but rather what you are hearing and how you are responding. For example, we can reframe a statement or situation and look at it a different way:

- a problem as an opportunity
- a weakness as a strength
- an impossibility as a distant possibility
- a distant possibility as a near possibility
- unkindness as a lack of understanding

If we change our emotional state in response to what we hear, we encourage others to be happier. When they are happier, we will be more positive and optimistic—and vice versa.

There are three main types of negative thoughts that are always mindful of reframing:

1. *Limiting beliefs.* A limiting belief is a thought that prevents you from accepting your full potential. These are the "I'm not good enough" thoughts. The consequences of accepting your limiting beliefs rather than challenging them are severe; you end up not achieving what you want. When you counter a limiting belief by reframing thoughts based on them, you weaken the belief and reduce the chance of it getting in the way of your goals.

2. *When you wish that something acceptable were better.* Have you ever had a great evening or vacation—only to feel that you missed out on something you heard your friends had done? Have you ever beaten yourself up in in those kinds of situations—even though you had a great time! Rather than letting your mind be filled with negative thoughts, take advantage of this easy reframing situation and enjoy the moment you experience even more.

3. *Specific problem areas.* These can often be related to limiting beliefs, but they don't have to be. If you are working on a specific area of your life—such as wanting to lose weight or getting another degree—you can use reframing to motivate yourself to grow and realize a significant achievement in your life.

When you get down to it, reframing is a mindful component of your thought process. Embrace the fact that you possess it—and then use it! You might not reframe everything, but you should try to whenever a good situation for it arises.

THE JOY OF BEING AUTHENTIC

We have to stand up for what we believe in, even when we might not be popular for it. Honesty starts with being ourselves, authentic and true to who we are and what we believe in, and that may not always be popular, but it will always let you follow your dreams and your heart.

—Tabatha Coffey

ecoming authentic is an individual mission since each person has their own way of being human, and consequently, what is authentic will be different for everyone. Furthermore, personal authenticity is highly contextual, and it depends on various social, political, religious, and cultural characteristics. The unique nature of everyone is best seen not in who they are but in who they become.

Becoming authentic is not an event; it is a continuous process. It involves knowing oneself and recognizing others and the mutual influence between individuals. If the quest for personal authenticity is just for self-fulfillment, then it is individualistic and based upon the ego-. However, if it is accompanied by the awareness of others and the wider world, it can be a worthwhile goal.

You do not need to tell a stranger your life story to be authentic. You just must be. Love yourself. Detach yourself from the outcome of everything you do. Be committed to yourself and to the process—and let go of what could, should, would, must, and needs to happen.

Trust yourself. Show up. Take risks. Reflect. Keep on trying!

Jennifer Ryan, MEd, LPC-S, has developed a successful practice in Allen, Texas, and provides a great list[3] of the ten characteristics of authentic people:

---

[3] Detailed text for each of these characteristics can be obtained on Jennifer's website: www.Ichoosechange.com.

- live in the present
- free of fear
- not judgmental
- generally appreciate themselves
- hunger for truth
- adaptable and flexible
- strong sense of gratitude
- love to laugh and lighthearted
- high degree of dignity
- sleep well

I like these characteristics and continually strive to embrace them. Remember, it is a process of becoming—and not just an event! Join the journey!

WHAT'S LIVING ALL ABOUT?

Life is a sum of all your choices.

—Albert Camus

W e are all in transition. So where are you heading?

- *Wandering*: For some people, there is no clear path to the next level. They are drifting in the land of wishes, desires, and dreams. There is no clear sense of direction, and when they are given the opportunity to gain knowledge from a trusted resource, they decline the offer! They are often stubborn to the point of failure—and many do end up failing!

- *Stuck*: Some people frequently find themselves just stuck! Fear rules their lives. They are unable to make decisions to change careers, mend or develop new relationships, or even plan for the future. Indifference is their mantra—and they are driven by fear. As a result, they are most unhappy with life! They seem to never move forward!

- *Living*: Some people live with purpose. They meditate on the good of life. They engage themselves in the lives of others, are grounded spiritually, stay connected, and are driven to explore new knowledge. They choose to make informed decisions, encourage others—and applaud them when they succeed—and accept challenges and learn from them. These are the people who are truly living!

IT'S ALL A MATTER OF CHOICES!

Choice theory, which was developed by William Glasser, states that we are the by-products of the choices we make in life. His theory is quite detailed and is the basis for reality therapy, which is frequently used by licensed counselors and psychologists. Our discussion here is to be reflective on the choices that impact our lives.

In Hal Urban's *Life's Greatest Lessons*,[4] we discover that we have the freedom of choice as we go through our lives. Our choices determine the quality of our lives:

> *We're free to choose our character—the type of persons we become.* We can allow ourselves to be molded by others and our environment, or we can commit ourselves to self-development. We can become less than we're capable of or we can become all that we are capable of.

> *We're free to choose our values.* We can let the media tell us what's important, or we can decide for ourselves. We can base our standards on what others are doing, or we can base them on what we know is right and good.

> *We're free to choose how we treat other people.* We can put them down, or we can lift them up. We can be self-centered and inconsiderate, or we can be respectful, kind, and helpful.

---

[4] *Life's Greatest Lessons: 20 Things That Matter* by Hal Urban. Reprinted with permission of Fireside, a division of Simon & Schuster, Inc.

We're free to choose who to handle adversity. We can allow ourselves to be crushed, to give up, and to feel sorry for ourselves. Or we can choose to look for a source of strength within us, to persevere, and to make the most out of what life deals us.

We're free to choose how much we'll learn. We can look upon learning as an unpleasant duty or as a great opportunity for bettering ourselves. We can be closed-minded or open-minded; we can be stagnant, or we can grow.

We're free to choose what we'll accomplish in life. We can allow our circumstances or other people to determine what we make out ourselves, or we can choose our own direction and goals. We can be undisciplined and lazy, or we can be self-disciplined and hardworking.

We're free to choose our own belief system. We can ignore our spiritual nature, or we can accept it as an important dimension of life. We can worship pleasure and the world's material things, or we can look for something that's ultimately more important.

We're free to choose our own purpose. We can wander aimlessly, or we can search for a meaning in life, and then live according to it. We can live to please only ourselves, or we can find a cause that's greater, one that helps us understand and appreciate life more fully.

We're free to choose our attitude regardless of circumstances. This is the most important choice we'll ever make because it affects everything we do in life.

The most important thing to understand about this is that, at any given moment, we're making choices.

You will never get out of life what you want unless you have a road map. Only you can chart the course and make meaningful choices as you go through your life journey.

Where are you on your life journey? Are you making the best choices that will give you the optimal opportunity for a meaningful and purposeful life? Think about these things!

WHEN TRAGEDY HAPPENS

The tragedy of life is often not in our failure, but rather in our complacency; not in our doing too much, but rather in our doing too little; not in our living above our ability, but rather in our living below our capacities.

—Benjamin E. Mays

NATIONAL AND GLOBAL TRAGEDIES

Words cannot adequately express how we feel when we experience extreme shock and sorrow. We are troubled when unexpected events occur that cause death and harm to many people. What we learn from such incidents is that, at the heart of most us, we collectively feel pain, distress, and emotional unease. Prayers are spoken for those affected. We wish that the incident did not happen. Could someone have prevented it? My sense is the answers lie within each of us. We have no control over what has occurred, but we can again seek to create a world where we are not so violent.

A possible solution is to really care about those who are close to us. Do not seek to divide but act in our mutual interest for a better and safer society. Create a society where weapons are not solutions and people and institutions that promote love and respect for humanity are encouraged.

In the end, we are the solution. What are you doing to promote unity, understanding, and peace in your sphere of influence?

PERSONAL TRAGEDIES

We all experience personal tragedies. When they occur, we may go through an emotional tailspin as we try to figure out what happened. Sometimes we are at a loss about what to do.

How do we go through these situations? Here is a suggested approach:

1. We must face the truth that an unfortunate event has occurred. Whether we had some control over the circumstances or not, it did happen. Emotional detachment is required in order to observe what happened.

2. Getting ourselves under control is next. Forgiving yourself and others involved helps immensely. It is not the time to blame others. What purpose would that serve? Also, it is not the time to jump to conclusions. It's time to assemble the facts.

3. Gaining perspective of what has occurred will help you overcome the tragic event in the future. You need clarity of mind and purpose. This is a teachable moment. What will you learn from it?

4. It is time to move on! Know your intentions. Take proactive action and move forward. Use the event as a catalyst for transformation and a change for the better.

Unfortunately, tragedies are a fact of life. Whether globally, politically, socially, or personally experienced in our lifetime, they will happen. The choice is how we respond to the tragedy, what we learn from it, and what is done to overcome it.

> Tragedy is a tool for the living to gain wisdom—
> not a guide by which we live.
>
> —Robert Kennedy

STARTING YOUR DAY

Gratitude makes sense of our past, brings peace for today, and creates a vision for tomorrow.

—Melody Beattie

W hat's the first thing that comes to your mind as you start each day? I need my coffee? Mentally going over all the things you must accomplish for the day? What will I wear?

You can probably relate to these common thoughts as you begin your day, and therein lies the problem. You have already set the pace for another stressful day. Try waking up and just being in the moment. Don't think of the busyness of the day ahead. Instead, try expressing within yourself how thankful you are. You have been given another day of opportunity, good health, food and shelter, and family and friends!

Enjoy the beauty of a sunrise or a foggy or rainy day. Kick back, enjoy your morning coffee or tea, just breathe, and take in the beauty of your surroundings. These moments early in the morning are all wonderful gifts of being alive. As a part of this reality, in the moment, pause, reflect—meditate if you wish—and take in the moment. You don't need to spend a lot of time; fifteen to thirty minutes is a good start. Then start to prioritize you day!

Rising early and giving yourself time to be in the moment each day will help guide you to be more focused and at peace!

Each day, rise and look around you. What do you see? What do you hear? Sometimes, silence is golden, and it can speak volumes to the soul. Each day is a gift to be cherished, experienced, and shared. Start it off right!

EVERYTHING HAS A PRICE

Everything has a price. Whatever we want in life, we must give up something to get it. The greater the value, the greater the sacrifice required. There are no options.

—Bill Blalock

verything has a price. Whatever we want in life, we must give up something to get it. The greater the value, the greater the sacrifice required.

Life is like a toll road! We all have experienced the reality of having to use toll roads. There is a price we pay for the luxury of getting to our destinations as efficiently as possible. Unfortunately, on occasion, there will be an accident on that road, and we will experience frustration before we eventually arrive at our destinations.

What's the point? Even paying the price for convenience and efficiency, we experience obstacles that we either overcome or work through. For every journey in life, to achieve some measure of personal success, we must pay a price in some form. Ask yourself these questions:

- What is the price of friendship?
- What is the price of forgiveness?
- What is the price of a new career or a new opportunity?
- What is the price of peace of mind?
- What is the price of a healthy lifestyle?
- What is the price of achieving new goals in life?
- What is the price of love?
- What is the price of appreciation?

You can add to this list—and then pause to reflect on what it takes to get what we want out of life. There is a price! What are you paying and receiving in your life?

CHANGE

Change is the law of life. And those
who look only to the past or present
are certain to miss the future.

—John F. Kennedy

Artificial intelligence, virtual reality, advanced manufacturing, coding, self-driving cars, apps for every occasion, and online shopping may sound like a lot—and they are—but these words encompass a major paradigm shift in our world and define the future, which is approaching quickly. I even have trouble managing my intelligent TV, which, in the future will not be HD but 4K and up to 8K and beyond. So where does that place you and me?

Change is constant throughout life, and we are fast approaching the time when technology is exceeding our capacity to manage change. This demands that we be very open to change and develop new skills and processes. Our lives will never be the same again, and we must accept change—not fight it! In reality, we probably will not have a choice!

As they say, the train has left the station! This is a good time to take inventory of where you need additional skills in your current career and look to the future in terms of what will be required of you in your current or future roles. In your personal life, use as many resources as you can to educate yourself about new technologies that are designed to make your life easier. It will be frustrating at times, but be patient with yourself. If you can't figure it out on your own, seek the help of experts and/or the internet—and do the best you can to learn and adjust.

Every day is a new day, and the next developed technology, device, or process is just around the corner! What are you doing to adapt to your changing world?

TIME TO REMEMBER

One day at a time—this is enough. Do not look back and grieve over the past for it has gone; and do not be troubled about the future, for it has not yet come. Live in the present and make it so beautiful it will be worth remembering.

—Unknown

B e anxious about nothing—and be grateful for something! Embrace the moment you are in and extend your circle of influence to share love, encouragement, and gratitude. We all have moments that are not memorable because they invoke pain and regret. Don't spend your energy on those moments of your life!

We all have memories and recollections. Our minds have limitless capacity for memories. We can remember years, dates, people, events, places, music, and food, but we may lose some of its strength due to lack of use. I used to remember phone numbers and addresses. Now with the advent of smartphones, the internet, and advances in technology, I have been conditioned to depend on them rather than my memory data bank!

Regardless of technology advances, memories are vital for human beings. They assist us in developing a sense of identify and belonging. They protect us by helping us remember previous hurts and dangers. However, they also give us a sense of hope as they move us to consider our lives and remember how certain experiences and events propel us to a better future!

Realize that you have more successes in life than failures. And today, as in every day, you can make memorable occasions happen! May you focus on what can be and not on what has been. Make every day count! Living life in the present will give you a legacy to remember!

DEALING WITH DISAPPOINTMENT

When we focus on our gratitude,
the tide of disappointment goes out
and the tide of love rushes in.

—Kristin Armstrong

n the context of the political landscape and the inability of individuals to act responsibly for the benefit of all, we have all been most disappointed at times by our country's leadership. We have also been disappointed by our own personal failures, including some self-inflicted ones.

With disgust, we can feel totally helpless at times. The resulting feeling is not a good one! So how do we process disappointment we seemingly all experience from time to time?

For one thing, stop the myopic focus on the situation! We tend to focus on what is right in front of us and lose sight of the broader context of our lives. As they say, this too shall pass. And it will! We just might have to endure a bit more pain before sanity again prevails and allows us to move forward. Don't focus on the negative what-if's; instead, set aside the grandstanding, sift through the chatter, get the facts, and understand that in the end, the right decisions will be made.

The feeling we get after every failure or unmet expectation is one of the worst experiences we can have. Disappointment is a terrible dose of reality that hits us hard emotionally. We experience disappointments when we weren't expecting things to happen the way they did. A single feeling can set off negative feelings: anger, frustration, sadness, hurt and more. Life is never perfect, and we are all bound to make mistakes.

Here are six steps to overcome disappointment:

1. *Express it*. Learn to let out your disappointment at the right time and in the right manner. It is not a display of emotion. Start by accepting the reality of your disappointment. Know that you are upset and know the reason why. Don't be ashamed to cry if you must. For some, it is cleansing to shed a few tears. Letting out your feelings is healthier than holding them back.

2. *Look at it from a different perspective*. Once you've accepted your problem and let it out, the next step is to ponder it from various perspectives. Ask yourself if this problem a long-lasting one. Can it be repaired? Can you try again? Will it take a little more time to solve than you had planned? Don't lose hope!

3. *Talk to a trusted friend*. Another way to get perspective is by talking to someone who cares about you. Confide in them and ask them what they think. If this is a person who truly cares about you, they will probably try their best to make you feel better by showing you a different angle to the problem and suggest ways the problem could be overcome. Simply sharing your problem will do wonders for you.

4. *Distract yourself*. Sometimes, disappointment is just a lingering feeling that needs to be overwritten by other thoughts to be forgotten. You've been beating yourself up over what didn't work? Enough is enough! Now, it's time to give yourself a break. You're not perfect! Who is? Go do something that makes you happy but does not infringe on the rights and pleasure of others. Try to bring something new and refreshing to your life.

5. *Express gratitude for what you have.* Don't hang on to what you've lost. Maybe the thing you lost could be replaced by something better. Focus on what you do have and what you should be grateful for. Think about your family, friends, children, and the individuals who mean something to you. Take time out to nurture and cherish the relationships that are near and dear to you. Be thankful for the number of ways your life isn't as difficult as it could be.

6. *Be grounded each day.* Focus on the aspects of your life that help you have a better outlook! Focus on your job, family, spouse or partner, friends, place of worship, and organizations that nurture and advance the best in you and others. By doing so, you will learn a life lesson of enriching your life and increasing your circle of influence.

Disappointment will come, but hope remains!

SUCCESS TO SIGNIFICANCE

The difference between real life and a
story is that life has significance, while
a story must have meaning. The former
is not always apparent, while the latter
always has to be, before the end.

—Vera Nazarian

Making changes to make a difference. Is it all really about what I want out of life? To feel important, loved, accepted, appreciated, and valued. What levels of energy will it take for me to have this sense of success in life before I can make a significant contribution to life—in other words, be significant?

To begin that process, I must come out of myself and begin to experience life around me. I can't be too self-focused. I must become transparent and take a risk on life. Am I willing to do that? Do I want to just take what is mine, be self-absorbed in my safe place—where I always find myself—and indulge in the wants of my desire and lavish in the needs of my prosperity? All too often, we choose the later because it is easier and safer. As a result, we do not grow or expand our life experiences. We become self-absorbed. We become complacent, browsing Facebook and the internet for hours, sleeping, reading on occasion, and when not otherwise active, watching mindless television or movies to occupy the space of time.

What's the purpose of my life then? Just to exist? Is it so I can do as I please and have a roof over my head, food to eat, and a car to drive. I don't want to be too social because that takes work, and after all, I am retired now, so why the effort? I just need me and my world.

Oh, I have my acquaintances. They are there when I need them. For companionship, a task to be accomplished, which I am not good at or someone just to talk to.

Effortless banter about the events of the day or past relationships or employment. I find myself retelling the same stories and recalling how life used to be and how the world has changed.

Yes, I have isolated myself from others. Nurturing old relationships, making new friends, and developing new interests is too much work. I might not be good at anything new anyway, and I don't want anyone to know my business. I am in control. I have worked hard all my life, and I deserve what I have now.

So what do you have? John Donne said, "No man is an island unto himself." We must deal with the ebb and flow of the ocean and the weather patterns that will develop over the space of time. You can be your own island, but over time, the shore will erode as the ocean washes the sands of time into its vast space. Fierce winds will damage your dwelling and cause you to fear that the storm may be too violent for it to remain. There will always be forces to deal with in your self-absorbed island of existence.

So you tell yourself that what I described is not you? Are you sure?

Oh, I forgot, you are "in control" of your life! Really?

BE STILL AND KNOW!

The real man smiles in trouble, gathers strength from distress, and grows brave by reflection.

—Thomas Paine

To be quite honest, I am tired of talking about stress! There are circumstances in life that create a horrible environment that promotes stress in our lives. I said promotes and not causes! You see, conditions in life set the stage for us to respond to the circumstances of life! I choose to be more reflective than reactive!

It is so comforting to just be still and know that I am a person of value. Through the process of reflection—with no distractions—I listen to comforting music to calm my spirit and enrich my soul. You can use any style of music that calms your spirit and creates a relaxed setting. Make sure the setting is right: in a room alone or taking a casual walk with your headphones on! This is *your* time!

When I exercise my right to reflect and meditate, I find myself more at peace with myself and with others around me. I do not expect other people to have the same values or thoughts and preferences. I only expect them to value life and relationships! I prefer to choose yes! I am at peace with myself and my Creator, and that's all that really matters in this life. When I am in that zone, I relate to others in my life in a more accepting and loving way. We all have that capacity!

Plan now to make time for daily reflection. You will enjoy the journey!

MOTIVATION: FINISHING STRONG!

A truly good book teaches me better than
to read it. I must soon lay it down, and
commence living on its hint. What I began
by reading, I must finish by acting.

—Henry David Thoreau

W hen I am visiting with a potential client, they often share all the books they have read about success and motivation. I applaud them for their efforts, but I focus on the fact that most of these books really say the same thing. The information is presented in a different textual format, but has the same content! Are you setting realistic goals based on what you have read and then acting on them?

You don't need to keep reading more motivational books and success books, attending more motivational meetings and conferences, and buying more motivational CDs, apps or additional digital media! The secret to success and motivation is within you! Once you discover what your core motivation is, you can act on your goals and make them become a reality. It is a process!

So, if you find yourself always reading and seeking sources for motivation and success and never seem to get there—ask yourself the ultimate question: Why am I not acting on the information I am reading and hearing?

First, the definition of motivation by *Merriam-Webster* is "the act or an instance of motivating, or providing with a reason to act in a certain way, the state or condition of being motivated or having a strong reason to act or accomplish something, something that motivates; inducement; incentive."

You need to understand what your motivators are. Here are some characteristics of a truly motivated person: You have a strong reason to act. You have to be totally focused and exude confidence in what you are seeking to accomplish. You actually love what you are attempting to achieve in your personal or professional life. Others believe in you because of your attitude and the actions you take. Your motivation is internal and is aligned with your belief system.

Critical people don't accomplish much. They are always judging and looking externally at other failures or lack of confidence. This is wasted energy, and motivators don't buy into complaining or judging. By all means, a motivated person does not blame others for their mistakes. They take ownership, review the reasons why the mistakes occurred, and press on!

Admit your mistakes. If you fall, pick yourself up and move on, always looking for the possibilities that lie ahead, staying focus and determined. Motivators never give up. They press on—even if it gets uncomfortable at times. As they say in some situations, "no pain, no gain."

Never stop learning. Individuals with professional certifications are required to obtain a certain amount of continuing education to maintain those certifications. Physicians are certified in a specialty in addition to being a general physician. If what you seek to achieve in your life has immense personal meaning and purpose, never stop learning.

Associate with others who share the same sense of dedication, commitment, and emotion. It is contagious. Surround yourself with others who share your passion. Motivators are movers and shakers. They always see the possibilities of what could be!

Like most people, I like finishing strong. You must start sometime to finish! Where are you in this journey? The time to start is *now*!

NEW BEGINNINGS

The heaviness of being successful was replaced
by the lightness of being a beginner again,
less sure about everything. It freed me to enter
one of the most creative periods of my life.

—Steve Jobs

ife is a series of new beginnings! We cannot go back to the past and start a new beginning, but we can start today so that we have a new ending! The task of change can be daunting, overwhelming, and fearful. Once we embrace the possibility of becoming what we desire in our lives, passion take over and drives us to act. Action is the key! We see the benefits of beginning the journey and our emotions begin to take over. We ask ourselves:

- What do I want to achieve?
- What is required of me?
- What am I willing to do?
- What will it cost me?
- What or who will I become?
- What difference will it make?

At the completion of the journey, will my life be different? Will I achieve the career I have always desired, experience the most meaningful relationships, increase my faith beyond all expectations, become closer to those I love and cherish, and find meaning and purpose in my life!

Like Steve Jobs, I have acknowledged the heaviness of the pursuit of success in my own life and the "lightness of being a beginner again" during my life journey. Yes, when I decided and took steps to make it happen, I was relieved of the burdens of my past and the freedom to enter the most creative and rewarding chapter of my life! It does work!

Are there any new beginnings in your life?

THE ART OF BEING SATISFIED

Satisfaction lies in the effort, not in the attainment, full effort is full victory.

—Mahatma Gandhi

Satisfaction is the way a person perceives how their life has been and how they feel about where it is going in the future. It is a true measure of well-being. It is having a favorable attitude toward life. Life satisfaction has been measured in relation to economic standing, education, experiences, and many other factors. Though we will have points in life that are challenging, but I am addressing is *overall* life satisfaction.

Here are some points for consideration:

- *Have specific goals.* A goal-focused life will bring a higher probability of satisfaction. The achievement of specific goals affects us in positive ways. Hope and optimism are essential elements in reaching and sustaining meaningful goals. Optimism always leads to higher life satisfaction, pessimism leads to the opposite.

- *Have a value system.* What is important to you? It might be family, love, or money or material items. It varies from person to person. Higher probability of satisfaction encompasses people who have social support systems— friends, family, or church. Those who value material items are found to be less satisfied overall in life as opposed to those who valued strong interpersonal relationships, according to research from the University of Colorado at Boulder.

- *Expand your social network.* "The greatest predictor of life satisfaction is your social network," says Shawn Achor, MS, author of *The Happiness Advantage* and founder of Good Think Inc. "So, if you want to enjoy your life, you have to create social investment."

- *Participate in activities that have a purpose.* Volunteer for a nonprofit or be active in your church or civic organization.

- *View work as an extension of your worth.* Value what you do, take pride in your accomplishments, and focus on what you contribute to the company you work for or the organizations you are a part of.

- *Have a strong commitment to relationships.* Nurture your marriage, children, and extended family. Be committed to the concept of a lasting relationship that extends the course of your lifetime commitment to each other.

- *Have an active religious faith.* Studies have proven that religious people are more satisfied with their lives than nonbelievers. For people who attend a religious service weekly, many were "extremely satisfied" with their lives. According to the *American Sociological Review*, religious people gain more life satisfaction thanks from the religious experience and the social network they build by attending services.

Being satisfied is relative to the impact of life experiences and the incorporation of the points I have expressed. Given a choice, we all want a satisfied life. How's your life?

WHAT IS YOUR BELIEF SYSTEM?

A passionate belief in your business
and personal objectives can make all
the difference between success and
failure. If you aren't proud of what you're
doing, why should anybody else be?

—Richard Branson

What is a belief system?

- Mental acceptance of a proposition, statement, or fact as true on the grounds of apparent authority, that which does not have to be based on a fact.
- Whatever an individual is willing to accept without direct verification by experience or without support of evidence, resulting in an assumption which is taken as a basis for action or nonaction.
- Actual set of precepts from which you live your daily life, those that govern your thoughts, words, and actions.

These are some definitions of a belief system. What is your belief system? Do you have one? To discover what and why we believe as we do, we must be brutally honest with ourselves. Beliefs are also choices. If you want to know what your true beliefs are, look at what you do and how you treat yourself and everything around you. Who do you interact with or choose not to interact with? Have you taken the time to review your belief system? Ask yourself these questions:

- Have you given any thought to the belief system you have?
- Did you make a conscious decision to believe what you believe?

- Did you adopt the belief system of your parents, your spouse, or someone else because it was what you grew up with or just wanted to do?
- Did your cultural surroundings mold your belief system? Were you socially motivated to conform to the norm?
- When you made decisions, were they informed—or did you just decide arbitrarily?
- If you made an informed decision, on what information did you base your decision?
- What was the source of the information? Was it tested for validity?
- Was the source of the information you heard from other people who profess some expertise in social, broadcast, or printed media or a convention, seminar, or place of worship?

Asking these questions will jump-start your thought process and help you evaluate what you truly believe!

Always test what you hear against facts and evidence! If I adopted the social herd mentality of going along with everything I hear, I would only be reacting to information rather than making thoughtful decisions based on facts. You will know what you truly believe when you can defend where you stand when tested. So what is your belief system?

STRESS MANAGEMENT EQUALS LAUGHTER

The only thing that stands between
a man and what he wants from life is
often merely the will to try it and the
faith to believe that it is possible.

—Richard DeVos

A smile starts on the lips, A grin spreads to
the eyes, A chuckle comes from the belly;
but a good laugh bursts forth from the
soul, overflows, and bubbles all around.

—Carolyn Birmingham

Always laugh when you can.
It is cheap medicine.

—Lord Byron

The continued stressors of life and the inability of our government to function responsibly at times can create uncertainty in our lives, and we can find ourselves stressed and anxious. Well, I have found some wonderful insight shared by Elizabeth Scott, MS, that will help you laugh your way through life!

Research has shown the far-ranging health benefits of laughter. While more studies need to be done, studies so far have shown that laughter can help relieve pain, bring greater happiness, and even increase immunity. One study suggests that healthy children may laugh as many as four hundred times per day, but adults tend to laugh only fifteen times per day. Read on for more findings about the health benefits of laughter and learn how to incorporate more humor and fun into your life.

STRESS MANAGEMENT BENEFITS OF LAUGHTER

- *Hormones.* Laughter reduces the level of stress hormones like cortisol, epinephrine [adrenaline], dopamine and growth hormone. It also increases the level of health-enhancing hormones like endorphins, and neurotransmitters. Laughter increases the number of antibody-producing cells and enhances the effectiveness of T cells. All this means a stronger immune system, as well as fewer physical effects of stress.

- *Physical release.* Have you ever felt like you have to laugh or else you'll cry? Have you experienced the cleansed feeling after a good laugh? Laughter provides a physical and emotional release.

- *Internal workout.* A good belly laugh exercises the diaphragm, contracts the abs, and even works out the shoulders, leaving muscles more relaxed. It even provides a good workout for the heart.

- *Distraction.* Laughter brings the focus away from anger, guilt, stress, and negative emotions in a more beneficial way than other mere distractions.

- *Perspective.* Studies show that our response to stressful events can be altered by whether we view something as a threat or a challenge. Humor can give us a more lighthearted perspective and help us view events as challenges, thereby making them less threatening and more positive.

SOCIAL BENEFITS OF LAUGHTER

Laughter connects us with others. Just as with smiling and kindness, most people find that laughter is contagious. If you bring more laughter into your life, you can most likely help others around you to laugh more and realize these benefits as well. By elevating the mood of those around you, you can reduce their stress levels—and perhaps improve the quality of social interaction you experience with them, further reducing your stress level!

HOW TO USE LAUGHTER

Laughter is one of great stress-management strategies because it's free, convenient, and beneficial in so many ways. You can get more laughter in your life by utilizing the following strategies:

- *TV, the internet, and movies:* There's no shortage of laughter opportunities from entertainment via theaters, streaming apps, and TV. While wasting your time watching something marginally funny may frustrate you, watching truly hilarious movies and shows is an easy way to get laughter into your life whenever you need it.

- *Laugh with friends.* Going to a movie or comedy club with friends is a great way to get more laughter in your life. The contagious effects of laughter may mean you'll laugh more than you otherwise would have during the show— plus you'll have jokes to reference at later times. Having friends over for a party or game night is also a great setup for laughter and other good feelings.

- *Find humor in your life.* Instead of complaining about life's frustrations, try to laugh about them. If something is so frustrating or depressing it's ridiculous, realize that you could look back on it and laugh. Think of how it will sound as a story you could tell your friends and see if you can laugh about it now. With this attitude, you may also find yourself being more lighthearted and sillier, giving yourself and those around you more to laugh about. If you approach life in a more mirthful way, you'll find you're less stressed about negative events. You'll also achieve the health benefits of laughter.

- *Fake it until you make it.* Just as studies show the positive effects of smiling occur whether the smile is fake or real, faked laughter also provides the benefits mentioned above. The body can't distinguish between fake laughter that you just start doing on purpose, and real laughter that comes from true humor. The physical benefits are the same, and the former usually leads to the latter. So, with more smiles and fake laughter, you'll still achieve positive effects— and the fake merriment may lead to real smiles and real laughter.

Laughter lifts the soul and brings a wellspring of joy! I'd rather laugh. How about you?

GOALS WITH BENEFITS

What you get from achieving your goals
is not nearly as important as what you
become by achieving your goals.

—Zig Ziglar

Have you ever taken the time to list your primary life goals in order of preference? Many people have never gone through this exercise and express that it is not as simple as they thought it would be. If you were asked to list your current life goals, what would they look like?

COMMON GOALS

- have a great career
- be a better person
- get married and have a family
- be financially independent and retire early
- have my own business
- have a healthier lifestyle and lose weight
- practice my faith more consistently
- go back to school and get a degree

These lofty goals will require planning and time. The unfortunate reality is that most people never follow through. It's easier to plan a vacation than it is to plan your life!

If the goal is overwhelming and no specific plan of action is in place, do we just give up? The list is basically a list of wishes, dreams, and expectations! Such lofty goals are very subjective, and they have different meanings based on personality and lifestyle. All the goals listed are admirable, but how can they be achieved?

Why don't people set realistic, time-bound, achievable goals that will improve their lives?

- *Fearing failure.* People don't like to fail, and they simply avoid challenging and attempting a goal to avoid the possibility of failure. They miss the fact that they may succeed, but they are not willing to take the risk.

- *Feeling no personal responsibility.* They are taskmasters. What they have always done works for them, and they are not willing to change. Even if their current situation is uncomfortable, they refuse to set a new direction in life.

- *Achieving things in life without setting goals.* Some call this the luck of the draw. Others call it chance. People convince themselves that they have made achievements in the past without setting goals. They feel that goals are not necessary.

- *Not knowing the value of goals.* Taking the time to reflect on what a specific goal would add to your life is a tough task for some, but it helps to acknowledge the benefits that support your goals. Knowing their value helps. How will it make your life better?

- *Fearing success.* This is an interesting position to take. If you achieve a goal that adds to your position, financial status, popularity, or attractiveness, you might not want the responsibilities and transparency that comes with that success. Frustration can set in because, without the successful achievement of goals that lead to success—however you measure that—you damage your self-esteem!

Do you relate to any of these reasons? Are you setting and achieving specific goals in your life? How important are goals to you? Purpose without priority is powerless! When you "purpose" to achieve goals, you set in motion the priority in which you will achieve them! Planning is essential

You can be working on multiple goals at the same time if there is a defined plan.

Here are some guidelines for goal accomplishment:

- Write down your goal or goals in a journal. If you don't have one, start one today!

- List the benefits you expect to receive when you accomplish your goal or goals.

- Develop a strategy—a road map—to accomplish each goal. What are you going to do to achieve your goal or goals? List actionable steps with a specific time to be achieved.

- Without specific and time-bound goals, you will have a high probability of not being successful. Be honest with yourself! Is the goal you are setting realistic for you! Knowing who you are, is achieving this goal within the realm of possibility?

- Record your progress in your personal journal. Track your progress. If you are falling short, state that fact in your personal journal and decide what you are going to do to get back on track. Always be honest with yourself. Remember that you are doing this for *you*!

- Once the your goal is achieved, celebrate!

- Determine what you are going to do to maintain the goal you have achieved! Record it in your personal journal.

- A better you creates better relationships, creates positive personal and professional development, and sets the pace for a better life!

It is important to achieve your goals, but maintaining and improving upon what you have achieved is much more important. Consistent improvement in your life will strengthen your self-esteem, and as a result, you will be a healthier and happier person.

Are you ready to begin?

MINDFUL EATING

Mindful eating is very pleasant. We sit beautifully. We are aware of the people surrounding us. We are aware of the food on our plates. This is a deep practice.

—Thich Nhat Hanh

ow we appear to others greatly influences how we are perceived. A healthy physical body is always attractive to others. Perceptions are not necessarily reality, but with a healthy lifestyle, we will attract the right opportunities. We have an obesity epidemic in our country that is having an impact on people's legacies. How do people see and judge you today and throughout your lifetime? Don't get me wrong. Judging is not a positive attribute; it is a reality! We need to be consciously mindful of our eating. We do not have an option!

Obesity is a major health problem for the United States and globally. The Institute for Health Metrics and Evaluation [IHME], an independent global research organization at the University of Washington, found that 2.1 billion people—nearly one-third of the world's population—is overweight or obese. An estimated 160 million Americans are either obese or overweight. Three-quarters of American men and 60 percent of women are obese or overweight.

We need to be very mindful of what we are eating and how we are living our lives. Unfortunately, a clear majority of men, women, and children—including nearly 30 percent of those under the age of thirty—are obese or overweight!

A primary key to address this situation is mindful eating. With permission, I share the timely findings and suggestions of Christopher Willard. A psychologist and educational consultant based in Boston, he specializes in mindfulness for adolescents and young adults. He currently serves on the board of directors at the Institute for Meditation and Psychotherapy and the Mindfulness in Education Network. Dr. Willard has published five books on contemplative practice, including *Growing Up Mindful*, and he teaches at Harvard Medical School.

Apart from the content of one's diet, which should be fresh and healthy, is the manner in which you address how you eat. These helpful suggestions will facilitate you being successful in how you respond emotionally to eating.

LET YOUR BODY CATCH UP WITH YOUR BRAIN

Eating rapidly past full and ignoring your body's
signals versus slowing down and eating and
stopping when your body says its full

Slowing down is one of the best ways we can get the mind and body to communicate what we really need for nutrition. The body sends its satiation signal about twenty minutes after the brain, which is why we often unconsciously overeat. Slowing down can give your body a chance to catch up to your brain and hear the signals to eat the right amount. Simple ways to slow down include following many of your grandmother's manners: sitting down to eat, chewing each bite twenty-five times (or more), and setting your fork down between bites. All those old manners are maybe not as pointless as they seemed. What are some ways you can slow down eating and listen more deeply to your body's signals?

KNOW YOUR BODY'S HUNGER SIGNALS

Are you responding to an emotional want
or responding to your body's needs?

We often listen to our minds first, but like many mindfulness practices, we might discover more wisdom by tuning in to our bodies first. Rather than just eating when we get emotional signals, which may be different for each of us—stress, sadness, frustration, loneliness, or even boredom—we can listen to our bodies. Is your stomach growling, is your energy low, or are you feeling a little lightheaded? Too often, we eat when our minds tell us to rather than when our bodies tell us to. True mindful eating is listening deeply to the body's signals for hunger. What are your body's hunger signals—and what are your emotional hunger triggers?

DEVELOP HEALTHY EATING ENVIRONMENTS

Eating alone and randomly versus eating
with others at set times and places

Another way that we eat mindlessly is by wandering around looking through cabinets and eating at random times and places rather than just thinking proactively about our meals and snacks. This slows us down and prevents us from developing healthy environmental cues about what and how much to eat. It also wires our brains for new cues for eating that are not always ideal. Do you really want to create a habit to eat every time you get in the car? Sure, we all snack from time to time, but eating at consistent times and places can boost the mind and the body and help with moods and sleep schedules.

Mindful eating means sitting down at a table, putting food on a plate or in a bowl, using utensils instead of our hands, and not eating out of a container. When you eat with others, you are sharing and making healthy connections—and you slow down and can enjoy the food and conversation more. We take our cues from our dinner partners and avoid overeating or undereating out of emotion.

When we put our food away in cabinets and the fridge, we also are more likely to eat healthy amounts of healthy food. Consider what's around, where it is, and whether it's in sight. If we limit eating to the kitchen and dining room, we are also less likely to eat mindlessly or eat while multitasking. When food is around, we eat it. And food—not always the healthiest—is often around at the holidays.

Do not shop when hungry—but the middle path applies here as well. A psychological effect known as "moral licensing" has shown that shoppers who buy kale are more likely to then head to the alcohol or ice cream section than those who don't. We seem to think that our karma will balance out and we can "spend" it on junk food or other less than ideal behaviors.

EAT FOOD—NOT STORIES

This is another tricky balance, and ideally, we can find nourishing foods that are also satisfying and comforting. Eating raisins can be a powerful exercise. We usually eat raisins as a snack, in small portions and in a very casual way. At times, one at a time. When we slow down and eat healthy foods like raisins, we often enjoy them more than the story we tell ourselves about healthy foods. You don't have to plan your food down to each bite, and it's important to be flexible, especially for special occasions, but be aware of the fact that you might be changing your eating habits at different times of year or during different occasions. When you do plan ahead, you are also more likely to eat the amount your body needs and avoid undereating and indulging later or overeating and regretting it later.

As we practice eating healthier and a greater variety of foods, we are less inclined to binge on our comfort foods and more inclined to enjoy healthy foods, ultimately finding many foods mentally and physically satisfying as opposed to just a few.

CONSIDER THE LIFE CYCLE OF YOUR FOOD

Considering where food comes from versus
thinking of food as an end product

Unless you are a hunter-gatherer or sustenance farmer, we have all become more disconnected from our food in recent years. Many of us don't even consider where a meal comes from beyond the supermarket packaging. This is a loss because eating offers an incredible opportunity to connect us more deeply to the natural world, the elements, and each other.

When we pause to consider all the people involved in the meal that has arrived on your plate—the loved ones (and yourself) who prepared it, those who stocked the shelves, those who planted and harvested the raw ingredients, and those who supported them—it is hard to not feel both grateful and interconnected. Be mindful of the water, soil, and other elements that were part of its creation as you sit down to eat whatever you are eating. You can reflect on the cultural traditions that brought you this food, the recipes generously shared from friends, or brought from a distant place and time to be a handed down in the family.

As you consider everything that went into the meal, it becomes effortless to experience and express gratitude to all the people who gave their time and effort, the elements of the universe that contributed their share, our friends or ancestors who shared recipes, and even the beings who may have given their lives to be a part of creating this meal. With just a little more mindfulness, we may begin to make wiser choices about sustainability and health in our food—not just for us but for the whole planet.

ATTEND TO YOUR PLATE

Distracted eating versus just eating

Multitasking while eating is a recipe for not being able to listen deeply to the body's needs and wants. We've all had the experience of going to the movies with a full bag of popcorn, and before the coming attractions are over, we are asking who ate all our popcorn. When we are distracted, it becomes harder to listen to the body's signals about food and other needs. With your next meal, try single-tasking and just eating—with no screens or distractions besides enjoying the company you are sharing a meal and conversation with.

So, while formal mindful eating practices may be what we think of when we look back on a mindfulness course or retreat, the reality is that we live and eat in the real world, which is a busy place. However, we can take the insights gained from our formal practice—slowing down, listening to our bodies, doing one thing at a time, making even small rituals, and considering all that went into our meal on a more regular basis—to bring more informal mindfulness to our daily meals.

Is it time for some changes to improve your health?

SIX WAYS TO PRACTICE MINDFUL EATING

MINDLESS EATING

- eating past full and ignoring the body's signals
- eating when emotions tell us to eat (sad, bored, lonely)
- eating alone at random times and places
- eating foods that are emotionally comforting
- eating and multitasking
- not considering where food comes from

MINDFUL EATING

- listening to our bodies and stopping when full
- eating when our bodies tell us to eat (stomach growling, low energy)
- eating with others, at set times and places
- eating foods that are nutritionally healthy
- when eating, just eating
- considering were food comes from

COMPROMISE: WHAT DO I HAVE TO GIVE UP?

Tolerance, compromise, understanding, acceptance, patience—I want those all to be very sharp tools in my shed.

—CeeLo Green

When we hear the word *compromise*, we may think in terms of what we are giving up. To a greater degree, when we come to a meeting of the minds, we should seek what is for the greater good. In effect, we are giving up getting something in return.

All ideas are not bad; they vary in degree and come from different perspectives. In facing a decision in life, there are usually options. You have choices. Each one will result in a different outcome. Some complement, leading to the accomplishment of a defined goal, and some do not! Whether it is personal, professional, or political, the same principle applies. Our motives should always be for the common good, preserving the freedoms espoused in the Constitution and Bill of Rights.

We are a society of differences, and we should seek the common good for all rather than the interests of a select few. After all, we are a democracy. To paraphrase Matthew 6:21: "Where your treasure is, that is where you heart is also." What we value in life, we are willing to invest in. Our treasure is our financial resources, time, and a commitment to work together in a community of diversity. The result is a better world in which to live!

We must listen, learn, and make the tough decisions for the greater good. Compromise is good when we all win. The journey may be tough at times—and we might not always agree—but we can be agreeable in the end!

> All government, indeed every human benefit and enjoyment, every virtue, and every prudent act, is founded on compromise and barter.
>
> —Edmund Burke

HOPE

Optimism is the faith that leads to achievement. Nothing can be done without hope and confidence.

—Helen Keller

Hope is the basis on which we look to the future, and it directly influences how we feel in the present. It creates a positive mood about an expectation, goal, or future situation. Hope also strongly influences a person's state of mind and affects their behavior. The feelings you experience as you look ahead in your life—imagining what might happen or what profession you might choose—can affect how you currently view yourself.

When we have hope, we always imagine a positive outcome. Even if the present situation is unpleasant, the thought of a positive outcome can reduce the impact of negative events or disappointments when they occur. We have the power to adapt in many situations and make it through difficult times. Those who are hopeful and optimistic usually make it through and look to the future.

Sometimes relinquishing hope is a positive. When a relationship is ending, we should accept that reality. With all the effort to rescue the other person and save the relationship, we are drained emotionally and feel defeated. We cannot control the emotions or the will of another person.

We must face the fact that when hope is not a shared hope in the relationship, the result will ultimately be the termination of the relationship. When that occurs, it frees us up to experience a new hope for a relationship with shared values, mutual love, and respect for one another.

Giving up hope is sometimes prudent in situations where directing your attention elsewhere is necessary to reach your goals.

Why do we let our yesterdays clutter our present path of progress? My past experiences do not define the present moment, but I can choose to allow that to happen! We are all on a life journey, and joy, pain, sadness, and disappointment are all part of living.

Don't be shortsighted to think that other people have it all together! We all have feelings, but not all of us have hope! Hope promotes restoration and healing in our lives. In some instances, relinquishing hope is necessary to point us in a new direction. Having hope can result in positive outcomes.

In terms of our religious faith, hope is foundational. It is internal, very personal, and relational. Faith in God gives us a supporting foundation in support of our emotional states of mind and future destinies. We feel and acknowledge that He is in control— regardless of the outcome. A strong religious faith will facilitate better outcomes in your life.

When a relationship with God is experienced and nurtured on a consistent basis, our lives are truly changed for the better. We begin to live! Take time to reflect, meditate, and accept the peace and hope that come when we connect with our Creator. Life will be less of a burden, and your outlook will take on a new perspective.

Hope is not seen; it can only be experienced as a present reality in life!

CRITICAL THINKING

Education's purpose is to replace an
empty mind with an open one.

—Malcolm S. Forbes

veryone thinks—it is in our nature to do so—but so much of our thinking, left to itself, is biased, distorted, partial, uninformed or downright prejudiced. The quality of our lives and whatever we produce, make, or build depends precisely on the quality of our thoughts. Shoddy thinking is costly—both in money and quality of life. Excellence in thought, however, must be cultivated systematically.

A well-cultivated thinker does the following:

- Raises vital questions and problems, formulating them clearly and precisely.

- Gathers and assesses relevant information, using abstract ideas to interpret it, effectively comes to well-reasoned conclusions and solutions, and tests them against relevant critical standards.

- Thinks open-mindedly within alternative systems of thought, recognizing and assessing, as need be, their assumptions, implications, and practical consequences.

- Communicates effectively with others in figuring out solutions to complex problems.

Critical thinking is self-directed, self-disciplined, self-monitored, and self-corrective thinking. Critical thinking results in living with a purpose, based on a critical assessment of all the options in the decision-making process. Make a concerted effort to stop the "react and respond" behavior in your decision-making process and begin to exercise critical thinking, which will lead to a higher probability of gaining new knowledge, changing your behavior, and having a more meaningful life

Avoid thinking simplistically. Think creatively and begin living with a purpose and a plan!

So what are you thinking these days?

PERFECTLY IMPERFECT

Successful design is not the achievement
of perfection but the minimization and
accommodation of imperfection.

—Henry Petroski

I t seems like we all seek a perfect world in a perfect space, but the reality is that the only thing "perfect" is imperfection! While I was reading Steve Maraboli's *Life, the Truth, and Being Free*, I was so impressed with his comment on this topic that I must share it with you!

> We have all heard that no two snowflakes are alike. Each snowflake takes the perfect form for the maximum efficiency and effectiveness for its journey. And while the universal force of gravity gives them a shared destination, the expansive space in the air gives each snowflake the opportunity to take their own path. They are on the same journey, but each takes a different path.
>
> Along this gravity-driven journey, some snowflakes collide and damage each other, some collide and join together, some are influenced by wind ... there are so many transitions and changes that take place along the journey of the snowflake. But no matter what the transition, the snowflake always finds itself perfectly shaped for its journey.
>
> I find parallels in nature to be a beautiful reflection of grand orchestration. One of these parallels is of snowflakes and us. We, too, are all headed in the same direction. We are being driven by a

universal force to the same destination. We are all individuals taking different journeys and along our journey, we sometimes bump into each other, we cross paths, we become altered ... we take different physical forms. But always we too are 100% perfectly imperfect. At every given moment, we are perfect for what is required for our journey. I'm not perfect for your journey and you're not perfect for my journey, but I'm perfect for my journey and you're perfect for your journey. We're heading to the same place, we're taking different routes, but we're both exactly perfect the way we are.

Think of what understanding this great orchestration could mean for relationships. Imagine interacting with others and knowing that they too each share this parallel with the snowflake. Like you, they are headed to the same place, and no matter how they may appear to you, they have taken the perfect form for their journey. How strong our relationships would be if we could see and respect that we are all perfectly imperfect for our journey.

WILLPOWER EQUALS SUCCESS

Willpower is one of the most important
predictors of success in life.

—Unknown

Willpower is the ability to overcome complacency and procrastination. It is the ability to control or reject unnecessary or harmful impulses. It is the ability to arrive at a decision and follow it with perseverance until its successful accomplishment. It is the inner power that overcomes the desire to indulge in unnecessary and useless habits and the inner strength that overcomes inner emotional and mental resistance for taking action. It is one of the cornerstones of success, both spiritual and material.

We need to restrain our impulses and resist temptation. We must do what's right and good for us in the long run—and not what we want to do right now!

In the 1960s, Walter Mischel, a sociologist, was interested in how young children resisted instant gratification. He offered them the choice of a marshmallow now or two if they could wait for two minutes. Years later, he tracked some of the kids down and made a startling discovery.

Mischel's findings have recently been confirmed by a remarkable long-term study in New Zealand, which concluded in 2010. For thirty-two years, starting at birth, a team of international research tracked a thousand people, rating their observed and reported self-control and willpower in different ways. They found was that, even after considering differences of intelligence, race, and social class, those with high self-control—those who held out for two marshmallows later—grew into healthier, happier, and wealthier adults.

Those with low willpower fared less well academically. They were more likely to be in low-paying jobs with few savings, to be overweight, to have drug or alcohol problems, and to have difficulty maintaining stable relationships. Many were single parents.

This case study further enlightens us to be very cognizant of our decisions in life. We need to draw from our inner strength and exercise restraint in areas of life that are not growing healthily. Build your own self-control by exercising it regularly in small ways. Learn to recognize signs that your willpower may be waning:

- Don't crash diet. Develop a new lifestyle of healthy eating!
- Don't try to do too much at once. Set realistic goals. Establish good habits and routines that will take the strain off your willpower.
- Learn how to draw up an effective to-do list.
- Don't put yourself in temptation's way, and if you it difficult to avoid, make it harder to give in. Use your willpower actively: plan, commit, and do!
- Seek to do those things that build a good character and healthy living—and you will have a higher probability of success in life.

How is your willpower?

ENDURANCE

Endurance is patience concentrated.

—Thomas Carlyle

an you run the race to completion and complete an important task or specific life goal? Life is a series of uncompleted tasks. We should have more completions than half-baked attempts. We usually associate endurance with sporting events, aerobics, and physical training, but it has a much broader life application. I relate this term to my grandson who is the best example I know of endurance.

With my grandson's leukemia diagnosis, the required treatments were not a cake walk. At the age of three, with years of treatment, he exhibited unbelievable courage, strength, and resilience as he fought every day for his life. His goal was to live! The good news is that he did win that battle! He endured to the end of his treatment and is free of cancer.

We, who are most fortunate to have our health, coast along, all too often exhibiting an undisciplined life. Check yourself against the following and see what your level of "endurance" is:

- Have I stopped bad habits that negatively impact my health?

- Am I focused on my goal when it comes to my weight?

- Have I given my best in my profession and/or the company I work for?

- In dealing with pain and loss, am I seeking professional help to guide me in recovery?

- Do I have the stamina to maintain the accomplishment or level of excellence I have achieved?

- In times of uncertainty, do I draw from my support network and spiritual resources—or do I just retreat?

- Am I moving forward in achieving emotional balance and peace in my life regardless of life circumstances?

These questions are good checkpoints to ask ourselves frequently. The more we endure, the stronger we become!

Hang in there!

BUILDING CHARACTER

Let us not say, every man is the architect
of his own fortune; but let us say, every
man is the architect of his own character.

—George Dana Boardman

We are developing our character every day—formally and informally. Daily life is the platform on which we build our character traits. These traits can be positive or negative. I defer to those actions that build strong, long-standing, ethically based character traits that will last a lifetime. If we let the environment and people around us be instrumental in that process, we negate the powerful impact of our ability to be the change agent and sustaining force in our lives to maintain the character we most desire!

We must emphasize good character awareness. Read stories about men and women who have positively impacted the lives of many people! Practice responsibility, truthfulness, and compassion in your life. Participate in training opportunities that instill, enhance, and encourage continued personal development. The more you think in terms of good character qualities and surround yourself with persons who emulate those qualities, the easier it becomes to make those qualities a part of your life.

Raise the standards of good character and lower the acceptance of bad behavior! Be cognizant of your attitudes, words, and actions. Once you have said or acted upon a bad character trait, you cannot get it back. The impression is lasting. It is difficult to change a negative perception. Think before you speak or act. How will this impact the other person or group? Am I grateful? Am I responsible? You have the power to control your attitude, words, and actions!

Acknowledge the good character traits. We love to be recognized—in a good way. Develop a habit of recognizing and praising good behavior. If someone does a good job. tell them. If a friend or an employee goes the extra mile, thank them and reward them. When you personally exhibit acts of kindness and benevolence, tell yourself how great that was! Positive self-talk is good! We need all the positive messages we can create and deliver in a world of negativity!

Significant benefits derived from good character:

- helps individuals reach their full potential—in knowledge, skills, and accomplishments
- enhances self-acceptance, self-confidence, and self-satisfaction
- increases productivity and accomplishments
- improves relationships
- benefits and encourages others
- contributes to success

What are your building blocks for a good character?

INTEGRITY EQUALS STANDING FOR SOMETHING

The supreme quality for leadership is unquestionably integrity. Without it, no real success is possible, no matter whether it is on a section gang, a football field, in an army, or in an office.

—Dwight D. Eisenhower

I am perplexed with all the political rhetoric we hear. During election cycles, we are constantly bombarded by the media—only to realize that it will not be over until we, as citizens, vote!

Integrity is a life principle to be cherished and practiced in our daily lives. Politicians have often set poor examples! These individuals often are not reflective of the caring American citizens who labor daily to make a living, provide for their families, and have faith and a strong sense of community and values! Regardless of politics or social standing, we all must exhibit integrity in life.

In a 1995 *Journal of Philosophy* article, "Standing for Something," Cheshire Calhoun argued that integrity is primarily a social virtue, which is defined by a person's relationship with others. They stand for something, and they stand up for their best judgment within a community of people trying to discover what in life is worth doing:

> Persons of integrity treat their own endorsements as ones that matter; or ought to matter, to fellow deliberators. Absent a special sort of story, lying about one's views, concealing them, recanting them under pressure, selling them out for rewards or to avoid penalties, and pandering to what one regards as the bad views of others, all indicate a failure to regard one's own judgment as one that should matter to others.

Having integrity also demands that while we stand firm on the mantel of integrity—what we truly believe in—we must have proper respect for the judgments of others!

Integrity must never be compromised. Having said that, individually, we need to live in a way that has meaning and purpose for ourselves and others. We must have integrity!

What do you believe in? Do you have integrity—or do you compromise your values? At the end of the day, integrity counts!

CONFORMING OR TRANSFORMING

Vision helps us see the possibilities of
tomorrow within the realities of today and
motivates us to do what needs to be done.

—Unknown

onform or be transformed? What would be your choice? If I conform, I give up my creative choice to think of the benefits that could be obtained from the choices I have. Free will allows me to judge the merits of the decisions I make with the facts I have available to me. If I just conform to what is expected of me, I set myself up for a lack of personal identity. If I only act, think, and respond based on the expectations of others, what is my true self? How do I renew anything—much less my mind and thought process? Renewing is becoming new again. Renewing gives us a vision of what could be! I have the capacity to change based on the thoughts and desires of my existence that drive my actions.

Why do we settle for the expected rather than the exceptional? I pose that question to myself all the time. As a result, I am constantly renewing myself, processing new knowledge, reframing life experiences, and building on meaningful relationships that add value to my life. The process demands that I be completely honest with myself and the expectations I set for myself. When I do that, I find every day a refreshing challenge. Every day is more creative and intuitive that the day before.

Are you conforming or transforming? I choose the continuum of transformation.

OVERWHELMED? DON'T HAVE ENOUGH TIME?

Learn to enjoy every minute of your life. Be happy now. Don't wait for something outside of yourself to make you happy in the future. Think how really precious is the time you have to spend, whether it's at work or with your family. Every minute should be enjoyed and savored.

—Earl Nightingale

I just do not have enough time!" Are you kidding me? Last time I checked, we all get the same allotment of time. Busy is not better. Busy is just busy. Caught up in a maze of technology? iPhones, iPads, laptops, voice mails, television, Facebook, instant messaging, Zoom, Skype, and multiple IDs and passwords are all part of our lives, which leaves extraordinarily little focus on developing meaningful relationships and accomplishing our goals.

We are technologically tired and worn out. Our minds are racing with multiple segments of data, our eyes are tired, and we feel we have no personal space. If you have children, that is an added burden along with managing a household and a budget. For the unemployed, there is the constant emotional journey of disappointment and dwindling self-esteem. And then there are bills to pay, demands on your relationship, and the lack of intimacy between persons that was once more meaningful. We hear endless rhetoric about a recession and disappointment in institutions that we depend on—our education system and our dysfunctional government. How is your plan for retirement? What retirement! Geez, how many people have depleted their savings, 401(K)s, and other sources to just survive? Are you leveraged? Do you owe more than you can ever pay off? Most people are overextended. How is your waistline? Have a weight problem? Have I said enough? What solutions should we consider?

1. Set SMART goals. If you feel overwhelmed and experiencing a lack of focus, try breaking it down into smaller parts. SMART stands for:

- *Specific.* What exactly needs to be done?
- *Measurable.* How will you track your progress?
- *Achievable.* It is realistic? Can it be accomplished by the completion date?
- *Relevant.* How does it fit with your overall plan or goal?
- *Timely.* When does it need to be completed?

People fail because they fail to plan. Using the SMART process is a good way to address a specific area of your life or profession that needs to be corrected or resolved.

2. It is time to evaluate your life Plan—if you have one—and make some changes! Change is difficult, but if you want some peace in your life and want to live longer, there is no other option. Take an inventory of how you spend your time and the choices you make. Stop this madness. You are the only person who can make this happen! Do not let other people, institutions, and external forces determine your destiny. Deal with facts and not fantasy. Stand on your own two feet and begin to do some healthy procrastination and make healthier choices.

3. Slow down and eliminate that "not having enough time" feeling. This will help you be more mindful of how you are spending your time. As an example, when driving in traffic, another vehicle passes you going extremely fast. They are determined to pass you and "beat the light" so they can advance to their destination. As you approach the next intersection, you notice that the light is red—and

the person who passed you a mile back is right next to you. With all that speed, he got no farther than you did. You were mindful of your destination, your speed, and the law, and he got no farther than you did. There is no need to speed through life. Be in the moment. Now is always here—and you will arrive on time!

4. Practice mindfulness. Focus on the present moment. We waste a lot of time thinking about the past, especially where we were not successful. The past is always time spent. Time in the present is all we have. Now is here. Be mindful of the time you have in the present to make progress in an orderly and efficient manner.

5. Discipline yourself! Take inventory of how you spend your time. What you will discover is that digital media and the internet are robbing you of precious, productive, and valuable time. Set limits on the use of social media and internet surfing. Use the internet with purpose and intent to add value to your life. Digital media can be useful, but more frequently, it is a disconnector.

In a world where we are able to jump on an app to order dinner, get a ride from a stranger, or even pay our bills, there seems to be a decreasing need for human interactions. Technology is a tool that has allowed countless advances in medicine, psychology, industry and more, but it's also allowing us to automate ourselves away from human connection and personal intimacy—creating more emotionally detached people that ever before in history.

—Lisa Strohman, JD, PhD

What are your solutions for sanity in a world of chaos and complexity? Remember that less is more in your life. Quality counts—not quantity. People are more valuable than possessions and time spent on the internet. You have more power than you think in managing your choices and uses of time. What are you going to do?

MEANINGFUL RELATIONSHIPS

A friend is the best gift we give to ourselves.
Friends are those people in our life with
whom we do not have any blood relation.
It is a relation of love and affection
towards each other. A true friend loves
us unconditionally, understands us, but
never judge us and always tries to support
us, help us, and give us good advice.

—Anurag Prakash Ray

D o you find yourself continually perplexed by why people distance themselves from others? For many of us, we practice gracious hospitality, are available to others to support them during difficult times, and honestly seek the best interest of others. Why are we in the minority? Thoughtful consideration of others is becoming rare!

When no words of appreciation or positive feedback occur, we find ourselves disappointed—and then the repressed anger hits us. Why did I take the time and effort to help this person? Why didn't they give me equal consideration? I thought I knew this person.

I will never again reach out to others to be a support and comfort during difficult times. I will not extend my professional expertise and insight to those who need my services. I am taken advantage of frequently. I cannot take this casual rejection and abuse any further. I am hurt. I am tired. What should you do?

1. Acknowledge the feelings you have.

2. Get the facts and make sure your feelings are genuine. If you feel used or hurt, acknowledge it!

3. Accept the fact that your perceptions were never reality. The other person never really intended to include you. You were conveniently used for their self-serving purposes.

4. Look to your husband, wife, or partner for understanding and support. If the experience is shared, listen to each other's take on the situation, learn from it what you can, and rest in the love and support from each other.

5. If your husband, wife, or partner is the offender, seek professional help, such as a licensed counselor or psychologist.

6. Accept the fact that some "friends" are *not* friends—and some relationships need to terminate.

7. Remember that an acquaintance is not necessarily a friend.

Any relationship that grows, matures, and lasts is collaborative, open, honest, and affirming. When it becomes a one-sided relationship, it is no longer healthy! Pursuing such people to "keep connected" will only set you up for future hurt and disappointment. Don't mix your positive life energy with negative, destructive energy forces!

Life does go on! Cherish those friendships that are true and affirming and move on!

What are you experiencing?

HOW INCONSISTENCY AFFECTS YOUR LIFE!

Mutability of temper and inconsistency
with ourselves is the greatest
weakness of human nature.

—Joseph Addison

W e expect consistency in our lives. It makes us feel secure, confident, and in control of our world. When things do not go our way or situations change in life, we experience what is known as "dissonance." Dissonance is simply a technical term for the cognitive, emotional, physiological, and behavioral state that arises when things do not go the way we expect them to.

One thing that frequently occurs when we experience dissonance is a state of confusion and interruption. We ask ourselves what went wrong. What did I miss? We may experience changes in our physical state. Our hearts race, our blood pressure goes up, and our hands get sweaty. Basically, dissonance is uncomfortable. It is the result of inconsistencies in our lives.

To get rid of dissonance we need to change the way we think. Here are some useful tips:

1. Deny it. Ignore it.
2. Overload good versus bad results. Remember all the times you were successful.
3. Change your level of expectation. If we expect too much, we set ourselves up for disappointment. Set realistic expectations.
4. Reframe or change how you see the situation. Change your evaluation of the thought and find the best possible outcome. Educate yourself. Get the facts.

These are just a few ways to cope with dissonance in your life.

One of the ways we see dissonance in action is by "selective exposure." Some people selectively expose themselves to information whenever possible. They seek out things they agree with and avoid things they disagree with. Even if the information they are exposed to is true and valid—and they can gain greater knowledge and understanding on a subject—they reject that opportunity. It is inconsistent with their thinking.

I challenge you to test your thinking and not be so narrowly focused on life and information that you miss an opportunity to learn, grow, and possibly change your thinking. Political posturing and rhetoric that seeks to defend a position that may in fact not be in the best interest of all is dangerous. Stereotyping and making rash judgments can be just as destructive.

May you learn more every day about what you don't know so you are more informed to make better decisions in the future about your life and relationships with other people and other cultures. Being consistent encourages better thinking and decision-making!

BECOMING SUCCESSFUL

Believe in yourself! Have faith in your abilities! Without a humble but reasonable confidence in your own powers you cannot be successful or happy.

—Norman Vincent Peale

n one of my sessions, a client was quite forthcoming and stated that he wanted to be just like Tony Robbins. He was obsessed with the need for recognition and was deeply entrenched in a state of self-pity. The fact is he will never be like that individual. His perception was not accurate for himself or the individual he sought to mirror. You can only be who you are—period! Each person is unique and gifted in their own special way

So how do we define success? It could be building a successful business, spending more time with family and friends, excelling in your career, or become independently wealthy. We each define success differently.

No matter how old you are, where you're from, or what you do for a living, we all share something in common: the desire to be successful! There are some basic strategies that will help you achieve success in life.

To achieve success, you must have a primary goal. And no matter what your goal is, you must establish and maintain healthy habits that lead to goal accomplishment. One reason why so many of us are unproductive and procrastinate is that we are waiting to feel like doing it. That feeling unfortunately sometimes never comes—unless we are prompted by a major consequence. Waiting to "feel like it" should never be a part of the success equation. Tomorrow never comes! Habits turn into routines, and routines make it easier to keep up with all the necessary tasks—whether pleasant or undesirable—to achieve success! What habits would you benefit from in your life?

> The most practical of all methods of controlling the mind is the habit of keeping it busy with a defined purpose, backed by a definite plan.
>
> —Napoleon Hill

REACT AND RESPONSE EQUALS CURRENT PRACTICE

All too often, we go through life just reacting and responding to whatever stimulus comes along: convincing commercials, in-store promotions, product placements, or endorsements. If the creative marketing works, we just respond and make the decision to buy or engage in each activity. Not much thought goes into the process.

INDIFFERENCE EQUALS THE EASY WAY OUT

For some people, it's just indifference. However, I call it the easy way out! You simply do not take any action at all. You remain in a career that is not meaningful or rewarding, you decide not to expand your cultural or religious interests, or you don't nurture human relationships. You just get stuck in a rut!

CREATIVE THINKING EQUALS LIVING WITH PURPOSE

Successful lives imply creative thinking, resulting in living with purpose and meaning. Action is a great restorer and builder of confidence. Inaction is not only the result of fear and inaction; it is the cause.

Perhaps the action you take will be successful—different actions or adjustments may have to be a part of the process—but any action is better than no action at all.

TIPS FOR ACHIEVING SUCCESS

Go beyond the norm. Think big. Think about the possibilities. Everything that exists today was once an idea that was the result of a vision driven by inspiration. This has been true since the beginning of time. In the beginning, God created—and the rest his history!

Don't be afraid to fail. Never give up. The very moment you give up, you miss the opportunity for success. Someone else will come along and create the very solution you could have provided, which would have led to substantial wealth and contribution to society.

Henry Ford, founder of Ford Motor Company, once stated, "Failure is simply the opportunity to gain again, this time more intelligently." Press on. Never, never give up! Be a person of action. Be persistent.

Find what you love to do—and do it! What do you have a passion for? Build on that passion, and it will pay off for you. It is a good practice to always chase the opportunity rather than the money. Great artists, accomplished athletes, and successful business enterprises did not happen overnight. They were birthed by passion and nurtured by a commitment to excellence—no matter the cost.

Practice the art of good communication. Getting along with others and building a network of professionals and personal relationships is essential. Avoid conflicts if possible. You may need to be open to compromise sometimes if it will not 100 percent conflict with your overall success strategy.

Believe in yourself. You have the capacity to achieve your desired success! Don't let discouragement stop you. Press on with determination!

Many people miss the countless struggles and failures that successful people experienced until one day—by chance or opportunity—they rose to the occasion and were viewed by their peers and others as being "successful." We all have periods of great accomplishment and success as well as seasons of disappointment. That's life!

Remember that you are all you have! You are unique, and you are here for a purpose. We all cannot be stars, millionaires, gifted speakers, national personalities, or leaders of countries. Success should not always be measured by notoriety in the public domain. The most successful people in life are those individuals who try every day to be better people—loving, caring, and mentoring others to a better way of life.

We only have a limited amount of time on this planet, and if we all just took the time to accept our differences and embrace our common bond—the welfare of our neighbors—we would be a better country and a different people!

Embrace who you are—and be the best you can become! You are a success!

LESS IS MORE

It must be obvious, from the start, that there is a contradiction in wanting to be perfectly secure in a universe whose very nature is momentariness and fluidity. To put it more plainly: the desire for security and the feeling of insecurity are the same thing.

—Allan Watts

M any of us are constantly striving for a sense of security in today's hectic, complex world. Controlling actions—whether by pressing, forcing, resisting, and the like—are the primary means we use to try to accomplish this goal. What we fail to recognize, however, is that the harder we strive for security, the more insecure we become!

"Controllers" fail to realize that the more they try to control, the more out of control their lives become.

Controllers:

- seek importance and appreciation

- lack self confidence

- are insecure

- have an unconscious want for power and recognition

- think they are gaining power only to learn they are overwhelmed and miserable

  All too often, entrepreneurs, organizational leaders, and managers refuse to let go and assign tasks or projects to direct reports and subordinates. There is the intrinsic fear that they can do it better themselves. By not delegating, they know it will get done. This is not a good move. That is exactly what causes persons in leadership roles to become overwhelmed and "never have enough time."

Begin to train and empower others to assume leadership roles! Spend time developing, delegating, and reviewing so you can be more visionary and strategic. Let others be more tactical. You will accomplish much more, give you needed "bench strength" in your organization, and allow you to promote the business more effectively!

Empower others in your life to join you in each task or journey. Don't try to do it all yourself. In so doing, you will gain the trust of others and gain more value in your relationships. It's only when you give up control that you can achieve more than what you initially expected.

Are you a controller? If so, you can change. Remember that less translates into more!

GREAT FIRST IMPRESSIONS

You don't get a second chance to
make a good first impression.

—Unknown

t has been said that a first impression is made within the first seven seconds. People take an immediate inventory of your smile, your handshake, and how you walk into the room. They are asking themselves if they can trust you. Maya Angelou said, "People will forget what you said. People will forget what you did. But people will never forget how you make them feel."

- *Appearance.* Be very mindful how you appear to others. They will evaluate you from head to toe. Always put your best foot forward. Body piercings should be avoided—and tattoos should not be visible.
- *Appropriate dress.* Be dressed for the occasion. Business casual is usually the best approach. Do not overdress to intimidate the other person. If it is a social occasion and appropriate dress is indicated on the invitation, dress accordingly!
- *Body language.* Your body language silently speaks volumes. A genuine smile, good posture, a firm handshake, and making eye contact go a long way in how people perceive you.
- *Mannerisms.* Lean into the conversation. Show interest in the other person.
- *Cell phones.* Turn them off!
- *Speech.* Speak clearly and confidently. Gaps or reluctant response indicate that you are not sure of yourself or do not know the answer to the question you are being asked. Just

say confidently that you do not know. Do not try to wing it! If you do, you will fail—and they will sense you are not trustworthy.

With every encounter, another person's impression of you is formed. First encounters are the most important because they set the tone for all relationships that follow. Whether in your personal or professional life, it is extremely important to create a good first impression!

- *Come prepared.* Be respectful of other people's time. Be on time. Know the agenda, the purpose of the meeting, and your audience.
- *Be authentic.* Do not try to be someone you are not. Do not oversell your qualifications or expertise. You will set yourself up for failure. You will fail to execute and deliver because you lacked the skill and necessary experience.

If you do not know the answer to a specific question, be honest and admit you do not know. Being able to lean into your weakness of not knowing shows that you are self-aware and confident about what you do know.

A follow-up text, phone call, or email to thank them for the meeting or opportunity is important. This shows that you are making them a priority and gives you one more time to thank them and express your continued interest in the opportunity and/or proposal. If it is a personal encounter, a text or phone call is appropriate.

If you are meeting a person for the first time as the result of an online communication or interviewing for a job, make sure that you are honest in the communication and follow the suggestions in this lesson. All too often, people portray an image that is not realistic. As a result, they set themselves up for disappointment and rejection. There goes the self-esteem again. Always refrain from such behavior. Honesty is still the best policy.

I realize that I am talking about using good old-fashioned common sense here, but a little extra thought and preparation never hurts. Make every first impression a great one!

LOVING AND LIVING

Loving oneself isn't hard, when you understand who and what "yourself" is. It has nothing to do with the shape of your face, the size of your eyes, the length of your hair, or the quality of your clothes. It's so beyond all of those things and it's what gives life to everything about you. Your own self is such a treasure.

—Phylicia Rashad

he first letter in the word *life* stands for love. People cannot love humanity without loving themselves first. Having a good self-concept enables you to love, lead, and accept others. As the scriptures so aptly put it: "Love thy neighbor as thyself!"

To say that you cannot love those who are different than you are denies the capacity of love within, especially when you profess to be a person of faith. This is the motivation that brings about a sense of peace and contentment amid of world of prejudice, hate, and bitterness. I encourage you to love instead of hate and embrace the love within that gives you that capacity.

Given that ability, you need to act accordingly! In so doing, you will have enriched your spiritual walk, have a loving spirit, project positive energy, and be physically healthier in the present moment and the days ahead. Practice a living love for all humankind!

THE VALUE OF FRIENDSHIP

The wish for friendship develops rapidly, but friendships do not. That such friendships are rare is natural … they need time and intimacy.

—Aristotle

We have many acquaintances. We tend to equate acquaintances with friends and claim that we have many—even hundreds—of friends. Social media is testimony to this fact. We have filled our lives with a revolving door of folks who serve a purpose for a while but vanish as quickly as they appear.

Harvard author and professor of public policy Robert Putnam argues that we are so distracted by technology and life in general that we do not take the time to search for true friendship or nurture it when it has taken root. In our increasingly isolated world, the notion of friendship has become watered down.

Marlene Rosenkoetter, dean of the school of nursing at the Medical College of Georgia, identifies these virtues of friendship: playing a role in someone's life, feeling loved, feeling good about yourself, and having a support group. We might align ourselves with Ms. Rosenkoetter's approach to developing healthy and lasting friendships.

We need to be sensitive to the distraction and lack of true connectedness that technology creates for us. Developing meaningful friendships is essential to a well-balanced and fulfilling life.

Make time for people who provide meaning and purpose in your life, and if they respond in the same manner, you are most fortunate! What are you going to do?

AWARENESS COMES BEFORE CLARITY

It is the unmanaged and limited nature of our personality that causes us stress, conflict and suffering in work and relationships. Thus, managing personal reactivity is fundamental to giving our work and personal lives meaning and fulfillment.

—David Daniels, MD

A s Dr. Daniels suggests, personal reactivity holds the seeds of our unhappiness simultaneously with our breakthrough for fulfillment. Central to the transformative process is self-observation. We awaken and strengthen our ability to hear and be open to the whisper of the inner observer.

Self-observation leads to self-awareness. It must be consciously practiced. It is fundamental to managing personality so that the wholeness of a person manifests. When we remember that we are more than our personalities and habitual reactivity, self-observation becomes a little easier. Discovering how much more we are than our personalities and habitual reactivity helps energize and strengthen our muscle for listening within and to select choices from the inside out.

Be responsive, be centered, and be in the present moment.

Being responsive rather than reactive compels us to notice. Noticing is the beginning of self-observation. When we catch ourselves in a reaction, noticing fear, anxiety, or uncertainty, as if teetering on the edge of a dangerously high cliff, we follow our first impulse to protect by stepping back. Instead of running away or being paralyzed with fright, try a *the art of the pause.* This new practice may be as simple as briefly closing your eyes and taking a deep breath. With another person, allowing silence for a moment can help you bring your attention to the body and your heart—followed by a request for a break.

Both methods help us be centered in our whole being. The art of the pause generates space to listen within, and it puts the brakes on our habitual reactions. As we listen within, the *inner observer* helps us respond based upon what is most important. Strengthen the art of the pause and experience more sustainability to be in the present moment.

Listen to the wisdom within through the art of the pause and see how your awareness deepens and expands for the most essential and most important response to life.

Listen and learn! What do you hear?

DO YOU HEAR WHAT I HEAR?

Listening is such a simple act. It requires us to be present, and that takes practice, but we don't have to do anything else. We don't have to advise, or coach, or sound wise. We just have to be willing to sit there and listen.

—Margaret J. Wheatley

A re you listening or talking most of the time? Most people overvalue talking and undervalue listening—even those in people-related jobs, such as sales—but the truth is that effective communication is not persuasion. It's listening! Nobody ever listened themselves out of a sale.

Abraham Lincoln said, "When I'm getting ready to reason with a man, I spend one-third of my time thinking about myself and what I am going to say—and two-thirds thinking about him and what he is going to say." That's a good ratio. Listen twice as much as you speak.

Stereotyping others can be a huge barrier to listening.

In most cases, perception is not reality. If I tell myself that the other person does not relate to me, I will tune them out and probably miss an opportunity to grow personally or financially. If someone takes their time to talk to you, there is usually a reason. Hear them out—and then decide. Tune them *in*—so to speak! I have always learned from people I do not agree with. You will understand their opposition better, validate your position, or even reach a compromise of understanding. It will be life learning for both of you.

Don't be preoccupied with yourself.

You are not as important as you think you are. Other's perceptions of us may be far from what we consider the self to be. So acknowledge what you don't know, be open to learning, and assertively defend what you truly believe in. When someone takes the time to call, send an email, or write a letter, respond in a timely manner—within twenty-four hours! When you don't, it sends the message that you don't really care or you don't want to listen to them. If you find yourself guilty of this infraction, make a concerted effort to respond to each form of communication you receive. In so doing, you will gain greater respect and credibility!

Much wisdom and understanding are gained when we listen to others. When others reach out to us, we need to respond. Effective communication is not an option!

EMPOWER YOURSELF

Your life is a novel, every day is a page, and you have the power to make the story beautiful and go the way that you want it to go.

—Unknown

L ife has a way of piling up fast. With the media predicting impending doom due to a financial crisis every day—and morning and evening news reports that primarily convey only tragedy, corruption, and disappointment—do you feel a bit emotionally drained? What about those who have lost jobs or fear losing them. How about your business? Are times a bit stressful? These external events do impact us, and the only way to counterattack is to use your best asset—and that is you!

SECRETS TO EMPOWER YOU

1. *Trade a smile for a smile.* Ever notice that when you smile, the response is a return smile! According to research, moods and the facial expressions they generate are contagious. Does a smile sometimes make your day?

2. *Smile more often.* Using your smile muscles tells your brain to shift into a more positive mood. Think of oil and water. They just don't mix—and so it is with a smile. There is no way you can smile and frown at the same time! Try it! Then keep smiling.

3. *Explain your successes and failures like an optimist.* An optimist keeps failure outside, assigning it to external circumstances that can be dealt with. When success occurs, the optimist attributes it to themselves. A pessimist, on the other hand,

makes failure internal, global, and permanent and assigns success to "mere luck."

4. *Stack your deck.* If you always compare yourself to everyone richer and in better shape, you will always come up wanting. If you think of everything you're glad you're not, you will find more satisfaction.

5. *Shift your focus.* You might not be able to stop depressing facts or negative thoughts from invading your personal consciousness, but you can choose not to dwell on them. If you focus on the positive, the surrounding negative energy will gradually dissipate.

6. *Surround yourself with positive energy.* Build a healthy support network of friends and associates who exemplify a positive, affirming outlook on life. You will feel the positive energy when you are with them! They will energize you to a clear sense of positive self-worth and accomplishment.

By empowering yourself, you can see opportunities in even the difficult situations that will help you move closer to your own goals and dreams!

FOCUSED FOR SUCCESS

Successful people maintain a positive focus in life no matter what is going on around them. They stay focused on their past successes rather than their past failures, and on the next action steps they need to take to get them closer to the fulfillment of their goals rather than all the other distractions that life presents to them.

—Jack Canfield

O ne of the primary reasons we do not achieve significant goals in our lives is the inability to effectively stay focused on the goal we are attempting to achieve. Certain steps have helped me and many of my clients in this area. A phrase I once heard has stuck with me: "Drifting thoughts get you out of the zone of effectiveness." That statement serves as the foundation on which I build the following steps in staying "focused for success."

- *Use time more effectively.* We all get the same amount in our "time bank." The last time I checked, there were twenty-four hours in a day! We need to give serious thought to how we use our time to add value to our personal lives and professions. Bill Gates, Mark Zuckerberg, Steve Jobs, and Michael Dell made significant use of their time when they began their software and technology initiatives. Today, they are regarded as men of great accomplishment and impact on our economy and culture. In the future, many more creative minds and innovators will rise to the occasion.

- *Set boundaries.* Challenge yourself to reevaluate how you use your time. Learn to say no to social occasions or meetings that don't add value to your life. We attend many functions because others expect us there, friends or family just want us to be there, or it's a matter of habit. Do some selective procrastination with your participation in activities and determine those that you need to eliminate. Focus on the activities that add value to your life and assist you in reaching your goal.

- *Practice visualization.* You must see it mentally, believe it is a possibility, and focus on the reality of achieving the goal. When you do that, you energize and program your thinking to continually focus on seeing the goal to reality. Following this practice of visualization increases the positive energy flow and supports your pathway to success. Close your eyes. Do you see yourself achieving the goal you have set for yourself?

- *Be accountable.* To be focused, you must first be accountable to yourself. Secondly, it is imperative that you share the goal and be accountable to at least one other person or support group. If your desire is to lose weight and lead a healthier lifestyle, you could be accountable to your physician, personal trainer, or dietician. In life issues, you may seek a professional counselor, career counselor, or a professional coach. Be accountable at each milestone you set for yourself as you work to achieve your goal. When you achieve the goal, others can share in your accomplishment and be a support to sustain what you have achieved. I always encourage people to celebrate their successes.

- *Be persistent.* Once you have started the process to achieve your defined goal, do not stop. Continue the process by implementing the steps I have shared with you. Be consistent in the journey. Success stops when you do! So, once you start, never, never, never give up!

Once you have achieved your goal, you must be cognizant that you have become a person of influence to others. You are defined as a very important person or a very influential person. Characteristics of a VIP include:

- *Vision.* You know where you are going. You exercise visualization and see within your mind where you are headed. The idea or direction is conceived in your mind. You plan, study, and embrace your direction until it becomes reality.

- *Integrity.* You display integrity with insight and intensity. How others perceive you is key. Where is integrity rooted? Your integrity is revealed in your private world—within you, your moral compass, and your God. It is what you stand for and defend!

- *Purpose.* Why are you here? This is the uniqueness of who you are and the fact that you are doing what you were purposed to do. Driven by purpose, you make a difference in your life and in the lives of others.

Drifting thoughts get you out of the zone of effectiveness. The best way to stayed focused for success is to stay in the *zone of effectiveness*! This is a mind-changing and life-changing process. When you have achieved your goal, you become a VIP. You make a significant positive impact on your personal and professional life and in the lives of others around you. After that, it's on to the next goal. After all, life is a process of continuous improvement.

HOW DO YOU APPROACH LIFE?

Everything around you that you call life
was made up by people that were no
smarter than you, and you can change it,
you can influence it, you can build your
own things that other people can use.

—Steve Jobs

Every day, we look at life from our own perspective. Two people can view a similar life event and react in totally different ways. It's not the event; it's how we respond to it. It many cases, it's a matter of attitude—and that's a choice!

There are three basic ways to approach life. They're three of the best choices we make and three of the best attitudes we can ever have. I can almost guarantee that the more you use these three approaches, the more success you will find in life.

First, think with an open mind. An open mind is the beginning of self-discovery and growth. We can't learn anything new until we can admit that we don't already know everything. The purpose of gaining more knowledge isn't to fill our minds; it is to open them. It helps us to see all sides, be more understanding, and be aware of our own limitations.

Second, think for yourself. Without any effort—or even realizing what's happening—we can turn our lives into exercises in mindless conformity. We go with the flow and let others do our thinking for us. It's like getting into a circle and following the follower to nowhere. Since the ability to choose is our greatest freedom and source of strength, we can't give up the right to choose our thoughts. We can choose our own thoughts—and our own beliefs, values, and priorities. We need to develop and appreciate our own character. If we let others do our thinking for us, we will never experience the integrity of our own minds.

Third, think constructively. Does positive thinking work? Not always. Positive thinking has a nice ring to it, but for too many people, it's just wishful thinking. Positive thinking must be accompanied with genuine belief. People who succeed in life don't just *think* they can; they *believe* they can! I prefer constructive thinking. Constructive thinkers are aware of negative ideas clamoring for attention, but they don't allow themselves to be dragged down by them. Instead, they train themselves to choose thoughts that build character and lead to personal achievement.

> Your living is determined not so much by what life
> brings to you as by the attitude you bring to life;
> not so much by what happens to you as by the way
> your mind looks at what happens.
>
> —John Homer Miller

MAKING THE CONNECTION!

The art of communication is the
language of leadership.

—James Humes

Communicating is an essential skill for an effective leader. It sounds simple, but it is quite complex because we all have our own ways of communicating. Sometimes we get results, and on other occasions, we are not as successful as we had hoped to be. Is there a standard that can apply to all levels of communication? The content can be the same, but the style in which it is delivered is completely a different matter.

You have got to touch the heart of a person before they consider you a leader. For example, Napoleon made it a practice to know every one of his officers by name and to remember where they lived and which battles they had fought with him. Get to know others who work for you and with you and your clients.

You can't move people to action unless you first move them with emotion. Do you have a passion for what you do? Is that passion or vision shared? When you are positive and excited about what you have to offer as a leader, others naturally follow. It's the heart-before-the-head approach. To connect with people in a group, you must relate to them as individuals. You are not going to be successful until you fully relate to each person. As a leader, it is your responsibility to initiate connection with your colleagues, employees, and clients. They cannot know about your heartfelt interest in them unless you take the first step.

The tougher the challenge, the greater the need to stay connected. It is a continual process. People don't care about how much you know until they know how much you care. Never take the position it is time to stop caring when the task or objective is achieved or the transaction is completed. Your success is dependent upon their success.

To lead yourself, use your head; to lead others, use your heart!

FEAR

I've learned that fear limits you and your vision. It serves as blinders to what may be just a few steps down the road for you. The journey is valuable, but believing in your talents, your abilities, and your self-worth can empower you to walk down an even brighter path. Transforming fear into freedom—how great is that?

—Soledad O'Brien

F ear is a very powerful force in life. Fear presents itself in everyone's life from time to time. It is natural for all of us, but it is manageable! Fear will either take you somewhere or leave you nowhere! You can start overcoming and managing fear.

Admit the fear you have and own it. Acknowledge what the specific fear is. Is it losing your job, failing health, a troubled relationship, failure, or simply the unknown? In most cases, I have found that the barrier to success in life is the fear of taking a risk: changing careers, making a life commitment to a partner, developing new friends or associates, becoming more social, or committing to a religious faith. Whatever it is, name it and claim it!

Write down your fears in order of priority. Getting them out of your mind and on paper will help you acknowledge them.

Take action. What is the one fear I am dealing with now? List the options you have available to overcome the fear. It usually boils down to self-examination and realizing the strengths and weaknesses that are the underlying forces of what you are dealing with.

Addressing the weak points in your life will strengthen your resolve to overcome the fear. It may be more education, new job skills, the help of a licensed professional, studying your religious faith more intensely and practicing it, making yourself available in social settings, renewing old friendships, or volunteering for a cause you believe in. Essentially, you must act to overcome!

When you take that leap of faith out of your comfort zone and cross the barrier of fear, you will feel a sense of relief and accomplishment! So take action! Overcoming fear will give you the freedom you truly want in life!

THE JOY OF LIVING

The happiness of your life depends
upon the quality of your thoughts.

—Marcus Aurelius

A happy life is a healthier life! Happiness is a state of life that we create within us. How we relate to life situations and process it in our minds directly affects our emotions and our degree of life satisfaction.

Psychoneuroimmunology is a branch of medicine that deals with the influence of emotional states (such as stress) and nervous system activities on immune function, especially in relation to the onset and progression of disease. It is a big word with massive implications to your health and well-being. The mind-body relationship is extremely powerful. How you think directly influences your health and well-being.

Here are some suggestions for happiness and health in your life:

1. Exhibit a life of faith and a strong religious practice.

2. A healthy diet and exercise program are required. Frequent walks and weight control are encouraged.

3. Practice quiet time daily to reflect and focus on the goodness of life. Yoga helps in many cases.

4. Remind yourself that setbacks in life are temporary. They only become permanent when you dwell upon them.

5. Have a regular physical by your physician and/or specialists. Knowing that you are physically healthy mitigates the stress of potential illness.

6. If you have a severe medical condition, positive thoughts and meditation with the added support of friends and family can facilitate a better outcome.

7. Practice daily an attitude of gratefulness. Overlook the negative and focus on the positive.

8. Cherish the true health benefits of happiness:

   - protects your heart with lower heart rate and blood pressure
   - strengthens your immune system
   - overcomes stress
   - combats disease and disability
   - lengthens your life!

Let your life be filled with joy, health, and happiness! Your thoughts are very powerful!

CREDIT EQUALS DEBT

Credit buying is much like being drunk. The buzz happens immediately and gives you a lift … The hangover comes the day after.

—Joyce Brothers

W hen we give people credit for accomplishing a task or making a significant contribution, that credit or recognition is positive. However, when we look at credit in a financial sense, it takes on a different meaning.

Managed properly, credit is a powerful tool for acquiring assets and providing the ability to do things that bring us moments of enjoyment and pleasure. However, credit lends itself to increased materialism in our lives. Excessive materialism negatively impacts how we feel about ourselves, our personal relationships, our life satisfaction, and our finances.

Credit is really *debt*! When you use your credit, you basically create debt, which is an obligation to pay. Credit transactions create some immediate gratification, but the abuse of credit creates increased debt, which bankrupts the quality of your life and your emotional state!

If you become enslaved to debt—working only to pay your debts and not investing in your life and future retirement—you do not win! Your legacy will suffer. It takes discipline to control this area of your life.

Be prudent and frugal in your spending. Do not be enslaved to debt with the use of credit. In so doing, you substantially affect your ability to have a quality life experience, your relationships, and the welfare of others.

According to a Dutch proverb, "Promises make debts, and debts make promises."

PERSONAL GROWTH

All life demands struggle. Those who have
everything given to them become lazy,
selfish, and insensitive to the real values of
life. The very striving and hard work that
we so constantly try to avoid is the major
building block in the person we are today.

—Ralph Ransom

W e need to be proactive in how we respond to life's circumstances. That requires constant self-examination of where we find ourselves in our personal lives, relationships, careers, and spiritual growth. If we do not advance the cause of improving our lives, we will find ourselves in a rut and not making the advances we hope for. It is hard work!

Being proactive requires planning. We must work on a life plan that has specific goals for personal development and growth. That requires us to take definitive action in defining our goals and setting a timeline for their attainment.

John C. Maxwell, in *The 15 Invaluable Laws of Growth,* says, "If we desire to grow and reach our potential, we must pay more attention to our character than to our success. We must recognize that personal growth means more than expanding our minds and adding to our skills. It means increasing our capacity as human beings. It means maintaining core integrity, even when it hurts. It means being who we should be, not just being where we want to be. It means maturing our soul."

Achieving worthy life goals builds character and is evidenced by personal growth. If we do nothing, we will not experience the personal and professional growth we desire in our lives. Here are some suggestions on how you can experience a positive life cycle of personal growth.

- Do an honest self-assessment. Look within yourself. Character matters.
- Admit what you don't know.
- Ask questions and listen.
- Be open to new ideas.
- Be teachable—and always be willing to learn.
- Have an attitude of gratitude.
- Serve others.
- Be passionate about what you do.
- Appreciate and validate the help of others who have contributed to your success.

To experience personal growth, you must be honest with yourself. Personal growth develops and nurtures a good self-concept, enriches your life, and builds exceptional character.

IMAGINATION

First comes thought; then organization
of that thought into ideas and plans;
then transformation of those plans
into reality. The beginning, as you will
observe, is in your imagination.

—Napoleon Hill

Y ou must see it to believe it. Look around you. Everything you see was once the product of someone's imagination!

The first step in the imagination process is *visualization*. This technique involves focusing on positive mental images to achieve a goal. A thought generates a visual image in your mind of what can be.

For example, you imagine yourself completing college, getting a new career or position within your company, creating a new product or process, or building your own business. You imagine—and see—yourself in those roles or the invention of a new product or process. You then activate your belief system within, convincing yourself that you can accomplish the goal you have set.

Your imagination is a powerful creative tool for effecting change in your life. Use it often to lift yourself out of the ordinary and into the realm of possibility. Define all the necessary steps to make your imagined role, task, or product become a reality. The limits of imagination are only those you allow the mind to create.

There truly are no limits to what your imagination can produce. It is always operative. So don't limit the possibilities of a creative imagination. Tap into it often—and see what changes you will benefit from.

INITIATIVE

Destiny is not a matter of chance, it is a
matter of choice; it is not a thing to be
waited for, it is a thing to be achieved.

—William Jennings Bryan

People fall into three categories: those who make things happen, those who watch things happen, and those who wonder what happened! Who are you?

You must take the initiative for things to happen in your life. It is always a choice! It is the ultimate enemy of procrastination. Without personal initiative, you cannot be successful. Nothing happens until you do something!

If you are looking for a new career opportunity or new personal or professional relationship, you must be persistent in the search. If you cease your drive—personal initiative—in the search, it is possible that at that very moment, you stopped the process and missed the greatest opportunity of a lifetime! Never give up!

Elon Musk, the CEO of Tesla, had more failures than successes and was even on the brink of going bankrupt in 2007, but he continued to work his plan. He continually took the initiative and overcame unbelievable obstacles. Today, we have the finest electric car on the planet, solar power, and hyperloops—and I am sure Elon Musk is not finished yet!

We always see the success achieved by individuals, but we don't experience the journey to that point in their lives. Everyone is on a journey. What is yours? Are you taking the initiative to set realistic goals, develop plans, and take action in your life? Maybe today is a great time to start. For some people, it may be time to pick up the pieces and begin anew! It's up to you!

FORGIVING YOURSELF

The people who did you wrong or didn't quite know how to show up, you forgive them. And, forgiving them allows you to forgive yourself too.

—Jane Fonda

W hen you forgive, you in no way change the past, but you sure do change your future.

You can take something positive away from every experience you have ever had. Even when you make a mistake or embarrass yourself, you can use that experience as a learning tool to help make you a smarter and better person in the future.

Negative emotions can serve a valuable function in influencing our behaviors. Shame and regret teach us not to do certain behaviors that may hurt ourselves or others. Often, we cannot fully forgive ourselves until we've digested these emotions and learned what we need from them.

On the contrary, if we don't learn from these emotions, we are more likely to repeat the negative and destructive behaviors from which they stem. Once we learn our lesson, change the behavior and move on.

When we learn the lesson behind our emotions, it's like a weight is being lifted off our shoulders. We no longer need to cling to shame and regret. We feel glad that it happened, and we feel like a better person at the end of the day.

We are not perfect. We are all susceptible to the same flaws and imperfections. Therefore, we should exercise forgiveness toward ourselves, our families, our friends, coworkers, and our acquaintances.

Forgiveness doesn't mean that we should continue a relationship with someone who has hurt us or disappointed us. Instead, it means that we sympathize with that person's wrongdoing, and we hope that they eventually correct themselves and find their way. Some learn, and some never do. But you can—it's a choice!

When we practice forgiveness toward others, we make it into a habit, which makes it easier to forgive others when we are in similar situations. We are a lot more like other people than we think. Once we recognize our commonalities as human beings, we become kinder and gentler in our judgments toward others.

Les Brown said, "Forgive yourself for your faults and your mistakes and move on!"

Forgiving is a key element to healthy living. Live well!

MAKING DECISIONS

Somewhere along the line of development
we discover what we really are, and then
we make our real decision for which
we are responsible. Make that decision
primarily for yourself because you can
never really live anyone else's life.

—Eleanor Roosevelt

To effect change in your life, you will have to decide. Are you more decisive or indecisive?

Let's look at what typically causes indecisiveness. The process often starts when we bug ourselves about missing out on something that we think would make us happier or provide a need we perceive. However, when we act on that desire, we sometimes experience buyer's remorse and immediately regret the decision we made. Why so much cognitive whiplash?

Much of our worry about making decisions stems from our irrational—and impossible—need for certainty. Obviously, making a good decision is important, but when we escalate that preference into an ironclad need to always get it right, we are indecisive and fret and worry about any decisions we make. Worse, we reverse decisions—and then we worry about that!

Major causes of indecisiveness include:

- We don't know ourselves very well.
- We carry internal conflict on what I want versus what others want from me.
- We exhibit sloppy thinking and too much emotion.
- We don't want to know the facts.
- We want a guaranteed solution.

Life requires us to make decisions every day. We need to be aware of the major causes of indecision and realize that getting the facts and not acting on emotion is the best course of action. We need less "react and response" and more creative thinking that is driven by living for a purpose! Corporations spend millions on marketing to influence our decision-making processes. For many of us, we just buy into the latest and greatest and not the best!

When we let others decide what is best for us, we are responding to what others want from us. Being decisive includes:

- educating ourselves about our options
- making realistic comparisons
- understanding what we desire versus what we really need
- accepting the fact that nothing is guaranteed
- realizing circumstances change—and that we can always make changes

Whether it's losing weight, making a career change, planning for financial security, getting involved socially, or improving your relationships, you will need to use creative thinking to make the best decisions. When you are indecisive, you place yourself in a rut and are not making progress in your life. You are not getting what you desire out of life! Decide to act in your best interest and not responding to what others want from you!

Being indecisive is a decision! Where are you in this process?

MONEY

You are your greatest asset. Put your time, effort and money into training, grooming, and encouraging your greatest asset.

—Tom Hopkins

D o you think money is a symbol of you, your life, your work, or your value? You surrender a big part of your life for the sole purpose of acquiring money! No one says, "It's only thirty years of my life that I am working for this company." Nobody says, "It's only forty-plus hours of high stress, highly intense work each week." Do you think, *It's only money?* or *I have to make a living?*

Well, the "only money" is precisely what you are working to accumulate. You have old tapes running in your mind from people who didn't know you better. They didn't know that currency isn't important. It is devalued. Thus, you are devalued.

Do you think your unconscious mind hasn't figured this out? Do you feel devalued, unappreciated, and frustrated that you have not achieved financial security! Money is not everything, but money is the equivalent of your life's work. Your life is worth investing in, growing, creating, developing. Promise yourself you are going to utilize the money you acquire to accumulate wealth. You will learn, invest, and contribute regularly to your savings and investments. You will ultimately do what you love in exchange for money, and when this happens, you will acquire wealth faster than you ever dreamed.

Treat yourself—remember that you are your money—with respect and value. In so doing, you will seek out competent professionals to manage the by-product of your life's work. Changing the way you think about money will change your life!

You are your best asset!

BETRAYAL

Tragedy in life normally comes with betrayal and compromise, and trading on your integrity and not having dignity in life. That's really where failure comes.

—Tom Cochrane

With the best intentions to help people, we often experience betrayal. What is consistent in that experience is the person who is the betrayer does not communicate their reasons for their actions. They do not respond to emails, texts, tweets, or written communication. The betrayer just avoids accepting responsibility for his actions. These sociopathic and narcissistic personality types are alive and well. Their victims are left asking questions: What did I do wrong? Did I say something that offended them? I have always supported and encouraged this person. What happened?

We will never really know. We only know our personal experiences with individuals, and we have no knowledge of the real emotional state of our friends and business associates. They will always complain, and they may speak ill will of you just to justify the hurt and pain they refuse to accept for themselves. They would prefer to transfer their pain to others. You become their target!

Be the person you are regardless of the behavior of others. By doing so, you can live with yourself and know that you are doing all you can be to be the best person you can become! There will always be evil people—and I strongly believe they will meet their match someday.

Always guard your heart. Be cautious but loving. Your character and good reputation will always survive the test of these attacks. In the end, good always prevails over evil—even though it sometimes seems unachievable!

Everyone suffers at least one bad betrayal in life. It's what unites us and makes us better people. The trick is not to let it destroy your trust in others when it happens. Don't let them take that from you.

Continue to the best person you can be! Nurture your trusting spirit—but be on guard!

HEALTHY LIVING

I believe that the greatest gift you can give your family and the world is a healthy you.

—Joyce Meyer

We all want to feel good, be active, be healthy, and be mentally alert, but we sometimes don't want to do what is necessary to facilitate the sense of wellness—physical, mentally, and spiritually—in our lives. It's just too hard. Well, it does not have to be that way. The following suggestions can help you on the journey to healthy living so that your legacy lessons will serve you well.

This section is not complicated, but you should apply them to your life to be effective! Some of the topics will sound familiar, but they are necessary. There is no substitution for healthy habits that result in healthy living.

EXERCISE/STRETCHING

Physical exercise is a crucial part of staying healthy, but many people make it difficult, cumbersome, and intimidating. You can have an exercise program schedule developed and supervised by a trainer or go outside and take a least a thirty-minute walk three times a week. Consider taking a yoga class or a group exercise class. Exercise in a group on a regular basis can be an enjoyable experience. You can make new friends and build healthy relationships with people who care about their health. At work, take the stairs instead of the elevator! Be active and stay active on a regular basis! Once you start, do not stop. Make exercise a part of your lifestyle.

HEALTHY FOODS

Dieting is a depressing term. "On again, off again" doesn't work! Instead of dieting, focus on slowly improving the quality of portion size of consumed foods. Make an appointment with a registered dietitian and have them prepare a food plan for you. It is a good investment!

Avoid foods with processed sugars. Try fresh fruit or a protein bar with fiber. Add fresh vegetables—not frozen or canned—as a part of your daily main meal. Steam the vegetables. Don't boil or fry them! Eat at home as much as possible. Sparingly eat at fast-food establishments.

ADEQUATE SLEEP

Lack of sleep is associated with many diseases, including obesity. Studies have shown that people who do not get seven to eight hours of uninterrupted sleep a night are more at risk to gain weight. Keep balance in your body's time clock. Go to bed every night at the same time and wake up at the same time every day. This routine will keep you in balance, and you will be energized and alert for the day ahead. Special events at times will get you off your routine—but get back to your routine as soon as possible.

GET IN TOUCH WITH YOUR SURROUNDINGS

Fresh air is good for the soul! Getting outside is a great way to get some exercise and relieve stress. Prepare your lunch some days and enjoy it outside of the office. Go for a walk or hike a nature trail. Break away from technology. Turn off the smartphone and leave the computer or iPad at home or in the office. Take in your surroundings without interruption. Relax and breathe!

HEALTHY PERSONAL HABITS

It only takes a few minutes to wash your hands! It is the best way to prevent spreading germs that cause the common cold, flu, and other viral infections. And as my mother always told me, keep your hands off your face. Touching your face frequently spreads germs. Also, do you ever wonder what you are breathing when you go to bed? Change your sheets and pillowcases at least once a week. As you prepare for bed, take a quick shower. That eliminates pollen and helps you relax and have a pleasant sleep experience.

MANAGE STRESS

Stress causes chronic inflammation in your body. It is the underlying cause of many diseases. Inflammation damages and irritates the joints, tissues, and organs, making it harder for your body to work efficiently. Stress also affects mental health and can cause cognitive impairments. If you have difficulty managing stress, consult with a professional therapist or psychologist who can help you with effective stress-management exercises. When you feel overwhelmed, get up and get out and take a break!

DRINK WATER

Dehydration is often mistaken for hunger. After you eat—or shortly thereafter—if you feel hungry again, drink water! Your body is signaling that you need hydration! Proper hydration is necessary for the digestive process and healthy skin, hair, and nails. Drinking too many caffeinated beverages throughout the day will cause dehydration. When purchasing water, always consider brands that have a high PH factor (www.alkalinewaterplus.com).

The effects of lemon water are amazing. Squeeze lemon wedges into a glass of water—with no sugar—and drink with your meal or anytime you are thirsty. Research by the National Institutes of Health links drinking lemon water daily to boosting the effectiveness of the lymphatic system. It strengthens the immune system, decreases uric acid in joints, eases pain, and fights inflammation. Lemons provide potassium and magnesium to support brain and nerve health, which improve mental clarity and focus. It also helps ward off the growth of certain types of cancer.

Water is essential to life, and lemon water enhances the quality of your life!

LIVE YOUR FAITH

Practice your religious faith on a regular basis. Attending services and special groups will:

- provide a support system, especially during hard times
- provide a shared social network with shared values
- provide hope and protect against depression
- strengthen your faith walk
- strengthen the family system and other personal relationships

There is no substitution for healthy habits that result in healthy living.

RETIREMENT REALITY?

I actually think the whole concept of retirement is a bit stupid, so yes, I do want to do something else. There is this strange thing that just because chronologically on a Friday night you have reached a certain age … with all that experience, how can it be that on a Monday morning, you are useless?

—Stuart Rose

You have finally arrived! Really?

The self-made billionaire Charles Branson doesn't think that retirement should be the goal. Instead, he thinks that happiness should be the goal. He has a point. Life is a journey is one of the most world's commonplace analogies, terribly misworded and misused. So much so, it's almost lost its meaning.

> Traditional systems of education have skewed the meaning of life [toward arriving at a destination] by placing too much importance on progressing through school and college to career. He makes the point further that far too many people live to retire and therefore cheat themselves of an exciting existence.
>
> —Alan Watts

> When I was five years old, my mother always told me that happiness was the key to life. When I went to school, they asked me what I wanted to be when I grew up, I wrote down "happy." They told me I didn't understand the assignment, and I told them they didn't understand life.
>
> —John Lennon

The point is this. We should never think that we have "made it" when we retire. Life is a continuum. When we reach the point in our life we call retirement, it is just the beginning. We have so many more productive and exciting years ahead of us. If we stop, we die emotionally and eventually physically.

> I've never thought work as work and play as play;
> to me, it's all living and learning. The way I see it,
> life is about striving and growing. I never want to
> have made it. I want to continue making it!
>
> —Charles Branson

There is a lot of living to do after whatever age you call a retirement. Choose not to retire from life! Choose to keep living and loving life! Happiness is the ultimate! How about you?

LIVE YOUR LEGACY

LIBERATE YOUR HEARTS FROM HATRED.

FREE YOUR MIND FROM WORRIES.

PRACTICE YOUR FAITH.

DREAM BIG.

WORK HARD.

BE FEARLESS.

STAY HUMBLE.

GIVE MORE.

LOVE UNCONDITIONALLY.

BE MINDFUL.

EXPECT LESS.

EXPRESS GRATITUDE.

ENJOY EVERY MOMENT.

LIVE YOUR LEGACY NOW.

ABOUT THE AUTHOR

Bill Blalock Jr. holds a bachelor of business administration from Methodist University in Fayetteville, North Carolina, and a masters in counseling from Amberton University in Dallas. During his corporate career, he held many successful management positions at Frito- Lay, Coca-Cola Enterprises Inc., Ernst and Young, and Cadbury Schweppes, to mention a few.

After leaving corporate America, he focused on his passion for the development and enhancement of individuals' lives through his professional coaching practice. His aim has always been to provide solutions for success in his clients' personal and professional lives.

Living Your Legacy Now! is the product of more than twenty years of working with men and women, enriching and inspiring them to new levels of achievement and self-worth. From his corporate experience, he gained insight and effective understanding of organizational dynamics, mentoring, professional development, and change management.

Mr. Blalock has helped individuals and businesses create and maximize opportunities by staying focused, breaking barriers, and enjoying a greater quality of life!

Mr. Blalock has written many articles, been interviewed by various media outlets, been a conference speaker and panelist, and been involved with workshops and individual coaching.

For information about Mr. Blalock's availability:

Website: www.billblalock.com
E-mail: bill@billblalock.com

Social Media Blog Posts & Videos:

LinkedIn: linkedin.com/in/bill-blalock-42851913
Facebook: www.facebook.com/billblalockauthor
Website: www.billblalock.com/media, www.billblalock.com/blog

Printed in the United States
by Baker & Taylor Publisher Services